IRIS MURDOCH

FOR BEGINNERS®

BRAN NICOL

ILLUSTRATED BY PIERO

Writers and Readers

Writers and Readers Publishing, Inc
PO Box 461, Village Station
New York, NY 10014

Writers and Readers Ltd
PO Box 29522
London N1 8FB

ISBN # 0-86316-401-3
1 2 3 4 5 6 7 8 9 0

Printed in Finland by WS Bookwell

Beginners Documentary Comic Books® are published by Writers and Readers Publishing,
Inc. Its trademark, consisting of the words 'For Beginners, Writers and Readers
Documentary Comic Books®' and the Writers and Readers logo, is registered in the U. S.
Patent and Trademark Office and in other countries.

Publishing FOR BEGINNERS® books continuously since 1975

1975: Cuba . 1976: Marx . 1977: Lenin . 1978: Nuclear Power . 1979: Einstein . Freud . 1980: Mao
Trotsky . 1981: Capitalism . 1982: Darwin . Ecology . Economics . Food . French Revolution
Marx's Kapital . 1983: DNA . Ireland . 1984: Black History . London . Medicine . Nicaragua . Orwell
Peace . Reagan . 1985: Marx Diary . 1986: Brecht . Computers . Elvis . Psychiatry . Reich
Socialism . Zen . 1988: Architecture . JFK . Sex . Virginia Woolf . 1990: Judaism . Malcolm X
Nietzsche . Plato 1991: African History . Erotica . WWII . 1992: Islam . Miles Davis . Pan Africanism
Philosophy . Rainforests . 1993: Arabs & Israel . Black Women . Freud . Psychiatry . 1994: Babies . Classical
Music . Foucault . Heidegger . Hemingway . 1995: Black Holocaust . Black Panthers . Domestic Violence
Health Care . History of Clowns . Jazz . Jewish Holocaust . Martial Arts . Sartre . United Nations . 1996: Opera
Biology . Saussure . UNICEF . Addiction & Recovery . Buddha . Chomsky . Derrida . I Ching . Jung
Kierkegaard . McLuhan . 1997: Che . Lacan . Shakespeare . Structuralism . 1998: Fanon . Adler
U.S. Constitution . 1999: The Body . Castaneda . English Language . Gestalt . Krishnamurti
Postmodernism . Scotland . Wales . 2000: Art . Artaud . Bukowski . Piaget . Eastern Philosophy

Contents

Dedications

To Kaz: I'm still amazed at my luck...
BN

To Silvina
Piero

We live in a fantasy world, a world of illusion. The great task in life is to find reality. (Iris Murdoch)

Introduction

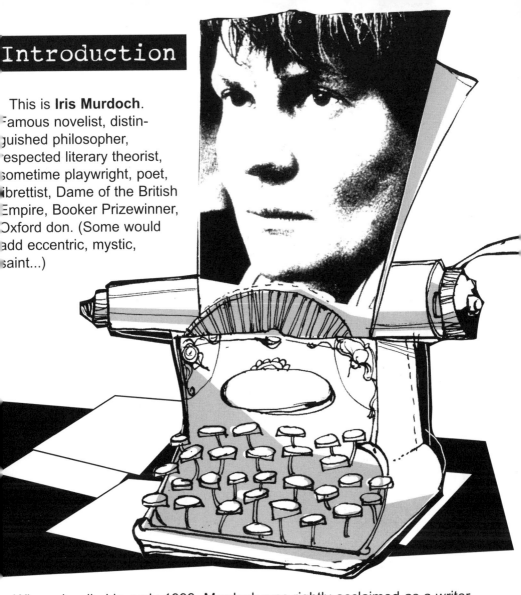

This is **Iris Murdoch**. Famous novelist, distinguished philosopher, respected literary theorist, sometime playwright, poet, librettist, Dame of the British Empire, Booker Prizewinner, Oxford don. (Some would add eccentric, mystic, saint...)

When she died in early 1999, Murdoch was rightly acclaimed as a writer who'd brought a new depth and direction to the British novel in the postwar period, and gone on to become one of our most original novelists. But her fiction is only part of a large, challenging body of work, founded upon a philosophy that says things few other philosophers have attempted to say in the twentieth century.

Iris Murdoch was more than just a writer. She was a thinker, equally at home in a number of different intellectual arenas.

This book is all about this extraordinary thinker... and her fascinating work.

Iris Murdoch
novelist

...WHO IS SHE?

IRIS MURDOCH BELONGS TO THE RARE BREED OF WRITER WHO ACHIEVED BOTH COMMERCIAL SUCCESS AND CRITICAL ACCLAIM AT THE SAME TIME. MILLIONS OF HER NOVELS HAVE BEEN SOLD ALL AROUND THE WORLD (ALL OF THEM ARE STILL IN PRINT) AND A GROWING NUMBER OF ACADEMIC STUDIES OF HER WORK ARE NOW APPEARING.

Visual proof of her singular status stands in the form of Tom Phillips' 1986 portrait of her in the National Portrait Gallery in London, where it is unusual to find portraits of living writers.

Many novelists make their names by producing one notable 'break-through' piece of work—a masterpiece, a *succés de scandale*, a work that captures the spirit of the times intentionally or unintentionally—no matter how many other great works they write. But this is not true of Iris Murdoch. No one novel stands out as being her masterpiece (though a case could be made for a number of them). Other novelists are successful because they're part of—or react against—prominent literary movements. But Murdoch belongs in a category of her own.

Yet it's not difficult to explain her success. To begin with, her novels are almost always exciting and entertaining. They combine
- the intrigue of the thriller,
- the twists and turns of the adventure story,
- the dark, brooding suspense of the Gothic novel,
- the quests and magical locations of the romance,
- the larger-than-life convoluted love-plot of the restoration comedy,
- the intertwined community of an intellectual soap opera.

But the thrilling, fantastic elements of her fiction are always combined with a realistic depiction of a detailed social world with lots of different people in it, reminiscent of the great Victorian 'classic' authors she admired (Tolstoy, Dickens, George Eliot). They're underpinned by allusions to Greek myths, Shakespeare, and the work of numerous philosophers. Her readers feel in touch with a powerful framework of ideas working just below the surface.

Murdoch's novels present us with an instantly recognisable world, which critics have called, imaginatively, 'Murdochland'. Murdochland is located in the fairly affluent areas of Central and West London, like Hampstead, Chelsea, and Portland Place. It's populated by eccentric obsessive characters who are civil servants or academics on the surface but self-styled knights on a quest for truth, selfless loving women, mysterious 'enchanters' underneath.

MURDOCHLAND

These people can seem very unlike the people most of us meet in our lives. (Even their names suggest this: Octavians, Lucases, Clements aren't too common in most parts of Britain.) It's true there are very few working-class characters in her books, almost no black people, but the inhabitants of Murdochland somehow represent every one of us, no matter our background. What's important is what they go through: the monumental experience of falling in love, the terrible consequences of being the victim of, or responsible for an accident, the desperate need to know that our lives have some meaning. These experiences are shared by everyone.

Early years

On 15 July 1919 Jean Iris Murdoch was born in Dublin, on the very street where the famous Easter Uprising had taken place only three years earlier. Though she moved to England when she was only one, and spent most of her life in those privileged educational institutions that have bred a great many English artists...

> IRELAND WOULD ALWAYS BE A 'ROMANTIC LAND' FOR ME, INFLUENCING THE CELTIC-INSPIRED FANTASY AND MYTH OF MY NOVELS.

> DEAR IRIS, HAVE YOU BRUSHED YOUR [ ] TEETH?]

Murdoch was an only child, existing with her parents in what she later described as a 'perfect trinity of love'. Her mother, a trained opera singer, and her father, a gentle bookish civil servant, instilled in their daughter an early appreciation of goodness... and a love of culture.

The books she read with her daddy, like *Alice in Wonderland, Treasure Island* and *Peter Pan*, left their mark on the novels she wrote in later life.

The perfect trinity was lonely at times, though. Around the age of nine, Iris Murdoch began writing stories in order to 'create' brothers and sisters to play with. Right away she knew what she wanted to do when she grew up. At fourteen her first published work, a comic poem, appeared in the school magazine.

At Badminton school in Bristol, Murdoch continued to write and deepen her appreciation of all things cultural: she learned Latin and Greek and developed a passion for learning languages. (Throughout her life she would curl up with books in French, Spanish, Italian, Russian and German.)

Her successful school career was capped in 1938 by winning a scholarship to Somerville College in Oxford to study classical history, literature, and philosophy.

OXFORD IS SO INSPIRING!

AT OXFORD THE AIR WAS THICK WITH THE POLITICAL AND PHILOSOPHICAL IDEAS SHE'D BEEN EAGER TO BREATHE IN.

Philip Larkin

She was surrounded by future 'notables' in politics (British Prime Minister Edward Heath), literature (poet Philip Larkin, novelist Kingsley Amis), and criticism (Marxist cultural theorist Raymond Williams).

The influence didn't only go one way, however. With her deep blue eyes and lilting Irish-influenced voice, one of her contemporaries said later, 'everyone fell for Iris'.

A different kind of challenge soon presented itself in the shape of World War II. While she was able to complete her degree (gaining a First, of course) Murdoch soon found herself in London listening to the bombs fall outside while she hid in the bath.

Finding the soap in the dark was the least of her difficulties. She was unsure what job she should choose—art historian? archaeologist?—and the instability produced by the war didn't make it any easier. But the decision was made for her when, for the early years of the war, she was conscripted into the Civil Service in London.

The war profoundly affected everyone who had to live through it, of course. This was no less true of Iris Murdoch. She faced common hardships like rationing and 'the Blitz'. But, on a deeper level, wartime and its aftermath led her through the key experiences on a personal, professional and intellectual level that would change her life and shape the course of her work. The most formative period of Iris Murdoch's life was undoubtedly the time from the end of the war to the early 1950s.

Formative years

At the end of the war Murdoch was moved to a United Nations post working in Belgium and Austria. The war left massive numbers of people without a home, or too afraid to go home. Murdoch had known a few refugees before, at school. Now she was more directly involved with their plight, providing them with food and shelter, sometimes even a new identity. Her work also included operating switchboards and, just the job for a philosopher, driving heavy lorries.

THE EXPERIENCE TAUGHT ME A GREAT DEAL ABOUT THE HUMAN CAPACITY FOR EVIL, AND WHAT IT MEANT TO BE AN EXILE.

She felt an affinity with exiles: her family were protestants in predominantly Catholic Dublin, then Irish people in England. Not surprisingly, political refugees frequently feature in her novels, and many other characters feel like outsiders.

A more exalted consequence of her experiences on the continent was the chance to meet an intriguing bunch of European intellectuals whose work would influence hers—and who also serve as models for the number of charismatic philosopher figures who feature in her novels.

They include: Nobel Prize-winning writer and thinker, **Elias Cannetti**, bohemian French novelist and, er, mathematician **Raymond Queneau**, legendary French philosopher **Jean-Paul Sartre**. Working for the United Nations meant that she had no time to read anything. But these encounters certainly gave her plenty to read when she came back. They also affected her choice of career. Back in England she decided to continue her study of philosophy.

Elias
Cannetti

At first she tried to do this in the United States, but was refused a visa because (like many of her contemporaries at Oxford) she had joined the Communist Party. Instead she studied philosophy for a year at Cambridge, under the supervision of one of the most eccentric philosophers of all (who lived a famously spartan life), the Austrian **Ludwig Wittgenstein**, before returning to Oxford to a post teaching philosophy at St Anne's College.

PASSPORT

As a young lecturer, Murdoch set the philosophy scene in the college alight. She ditched the stuffy, dry English philosophy fashionable at the time in favour of the juicy continental variety she'd come into contact with abroad.

WHAT DO THESE GUYS SEE IN HER?

I THINK I'M FALLING IN LOVE... WITH PHILOSOPHY.

If that wasn't enough, half the students seemed to fall in love with her. ('Seemed to'—because some would recall her later as a well-dressed blue-eyed buxom babe... some as a frumpy bluestocking in tweed skirt and woolly jumper.)

The war also meant personal tragedy touched Iris Murdoch directly. As an undergraduate she'd fallen in love with poet and fellow classical scholar **Frank Thompson**. Though his preference for the quiet scholarly life and his hatred of violence were strong, stronger was his sense of principle and he signed up to fight fascism at the beginning of the war. In 1944 he was captured in Bulgaria. He refused to collaborate and was executed in cold blood at the age of 24. His last act was to shout...

...I GIVE YOU THE SALUTE OF FREEDOM!

In his pocket was a volume of poetry by the ancient love poet Catullus and a Byzantine coin. Both were shipped back to Iris Murdoch.

As if this wasn't painful enough, Murdoch's next lover was also a victim of the war. **Franz Steiner** was a Czech-Jewish refugee, another poet, and like Murdoch, an Oxford lecturer. He'd always been prone to illness, and never recovered from a heart attack in 1948 brought on by the death of both his parents in a concentration camp. He died in 1952. The two deaths, in such close proximity, must have been heartbreaking for Iris Murdoch. It's not surprising that she was able to write so powerfully about love and loss in her fiction.

Murdoch wasn't the kind of writer to use her work as therapy, and her novels are never obviously autobiographical, but there's no doubt that her early fiction was shaped by her experiences during and after the war. In the late 1940s and early 1950s she'd been working on a novel called **The Flight from the Enchanter**, which features a scholar, reminiscent of Franz Steiner, writing a history of the Jews and a cast full of political refugees.

The Flight from the Enchanter was eventually published in 1956. Its characters are either in flight from political oppression or want to escape because they feel imprisoned. Responsible for much of this is a charismatic, slightly demonic figure called Mischa Fox—the enchanter—who manages to control the lives of everyone around him, while they worship him in return. Such a person will crop up repeatedly in Murdoch's novels. Her interest in enchanters, and the way they maintain power, was increased by her experience of the political realities of her time: how could fanatics like Hitler and Stalin manipulate the lives of so many and be loved and obeyed in return?

The next novel Murdoch wrote was actually the first to be published. **Under the Net** appeared in 1954 and was also concerned with imprisonment and escape. Its bohemian hero and narrator Jake Donahue is a kind of refugee through choice, rejecting the conventions of society, getting involved in a series of comic capers—being locked inside a flat, accidentally stealing a famous film dog, being chased around a gigantic film-set of ancient Rome.

It was an immediate success, and critics saw its author as part of a promising new generation of writers. Because of its rebellious hero critics included Murdoch in a group of writers (like **Kingsley Amis** and **John Wain**) whose work expressed disillusionment with 'the system': 'The Angry Young Men'. It was a strange label for a 35-year-old woman who was, well, quite nice really. What's more, *Under the Net* was about disillusionment at a deeper, more *philosophical* level than simply a youthful desire to get away.

Jake is involved in a kind of 'quest for truth', which says a great deal about the time in which the novel was written, and also about its author. For at the same time as the novel was published, Murdoch was busy working on an original contribution to philosophy...

What is 'liberal humanism' and why is it in crisis?

Britain, early 1950s. Iris Murdoch has been affected by the death of not one but two lovers, come face to face with the terrible suffering and political uncertainty that resulted from the war, but has been inspired by new intellectual possibilities and a sense of her own vocation. Ringing in her ears is perhaps the phrase Frank Thompson used in one of his last letters to her:

'WE MUST BUILD OUR WHOLE LIFE ANEW'.

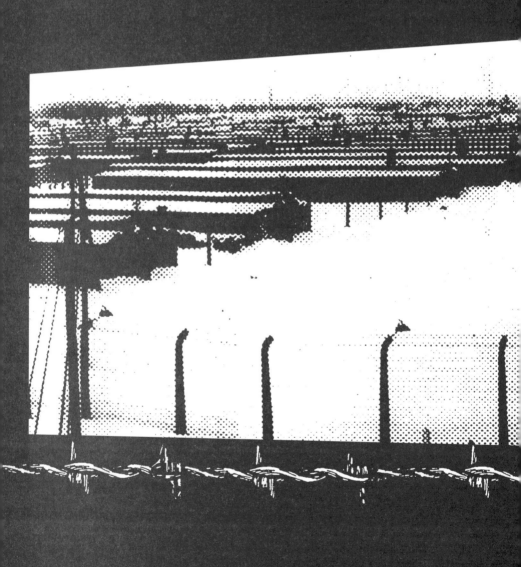

For this is what the whole of the country is crying out for at this time. European civilisation seems to be in ruin. The war has not ended humanity, as some feared it might, but it has ended almost everything else. The Empire is doomed, politics is seen to have failed, religion seems to be in terminal decline. Even art seems to be dying: the philosopher Theodor Adorno proclaims that Auschwitz has caused the 'death of poetry', critics are suggesting the novel is dead too.

Another major casualty of the war is philosophy. In particular, **liberal humanism**, the dominant form of thinking in Europe for the last two centuries, limps along, severely wounded. Liberal humanism has long maintained a faith in three related things:

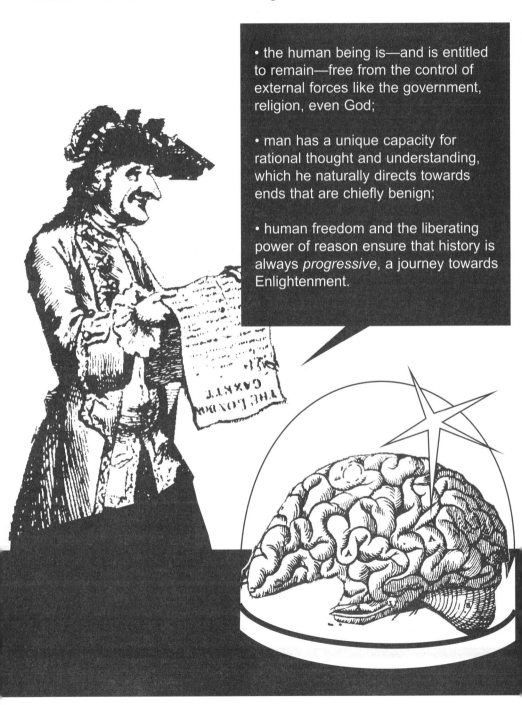

• the human being is—and is entitled to remain—free from the control of external forces like the government, religion, even God;

• man has a unique capacity for rational thought and understanding, which he naturally directs towards ends that are chiefly benign;

• human freedom and the liberating power of reason ensure that history is always *progressive*, a journey towards Enlightenment.

It is liberal humanism that has produced Britain's political system and its society, its literature and its thought. And now it is seriously in question. How can we maintain that human nature is fundamentally good after Hitler? How can we believe that human reason is well-meaning after the concentration camp and the H-bomb? How can we believe in progress?

In post-war Britain, then, besides the urgent task of changing politics and rebuilding society, there's a need to *rethink* this conception of the human being and his relationship with the world around him.

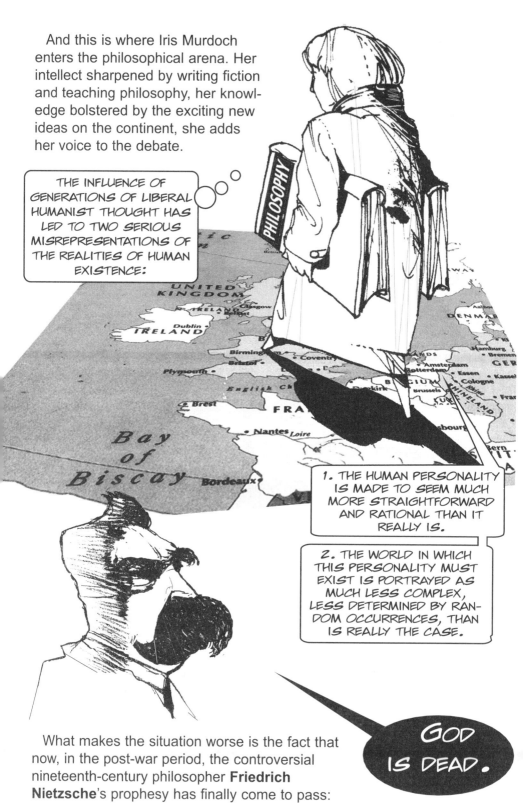

And this is where Iris Murdoch enters the philosophical arena. Her intellect sharpened by writing fiction and teaching philosophy, her knowledge bolstered by the exciting new ideas on the continent, she adds her voice to the debate.

THE INFLUENCE OF GENERATIONS OF LIBERAL HUMANIST THOUGHT HAS LED TO TWO SERIOUS MISREPRESENTATIONS OF THE REALITIES OF HUMAN EXISTENCE:

1. THE HUMAN PERSONALITY IS MADE TO SEEM MUCH MORE STRAIGHTFORWARD AND RATIONAL THAN IT REALLY IS.

2. THE WORLD IN WHICH THIS PERSONALITY MUST EXIST IS PORTRAYED AS MUCH LESS COMPLEX, LESS DETERMINED BY RANDOM OCCURRENCES, THAN IS REALLY THE CASE.

What makes the situation worse is the fact that now, in the post-war period, the controversial nineteenth-century philosopher **Friedrich Nietzsche**'s prophesy has finally come to pass:

GOD IS DEAD.

From the start religion was very important in Iris Murdoch's thought.

YET I WASN'T A RELIGIOUS THINKER IN THE SENSE OF PRESSING HOME A PARTICULAR CHRISTIAN OR CATHOLIC MESSAGE

I GREW UP AS AN AGNOSTIC.

I RECOGNIZED THE IMPORTANCE OF RELIGION AS A KIND OF PHILOSOPHICAL SYSTEM THAT HAD, FOR CENTURIES, HELPED US TO UNDERSTAND THE WORLD AND OUR PLACE IN IT, REMINDING US WE'RE NOT THE MOST IMPORTANT THING IN THE WORLD.

Religion teaches us about the mystery at the heart of humanity and in the world. It puts us in touch with something 'other', something divine, something that's in the world but resists our attempts to understand it. What's more, religion has provided necessary moral and intellectual guidance to our lives—it's a way of convincing us that our lives are meaningful, and that there are consequences to our actions.

But in the second half of the twentieth century, this philosophical system was collapsing, causing a major shift in the way we think about ourselves and the world.Once man looks around him and begins to suspect that the system that has been holding him up all this time is false, what does he do? The natural response is to retreat within the self—to say that the only thing he can be sure of is what he thinks, what he is able to perceive.

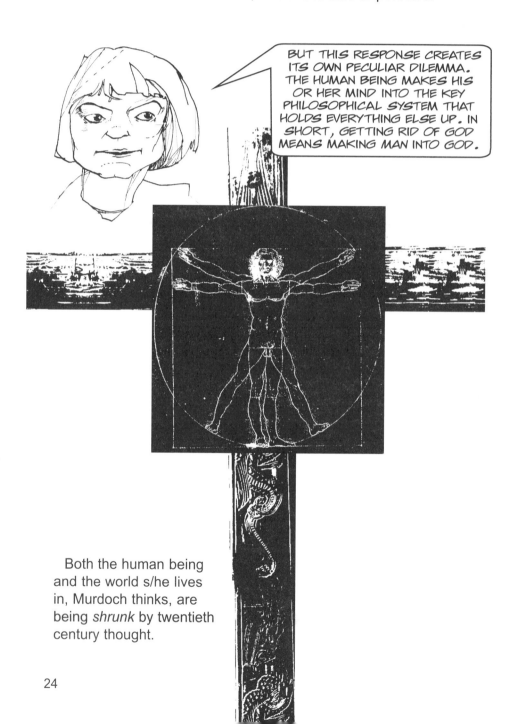

BUT THIS RESPONSE CREATES ITS OWN PECULIAR DILEMMA. THE HUMAN BEING MAKES HIS OR HER MIND INTO THE KEY PHILOSOPHICAL SYSTEM THAT HOLDS EVERYTHING ELSE UP. IN SHORT, GETTING RID OF GOD MEANS MAKING MAN INTO GOD.

Both the human being and the world s/he lives in, Murdoch thinks, are being *shrunk* by twentieth century thought.

1950s British philosophy (dominated by uninspiring things called **logical positivism and linguistic philosophy**) placed too much faith in logic and scientific method. It had little to say about those areas of life not analysable by scientific methods—things, that is, like the 'big' concepts philosophers are supposed to discuss, like 'identity' or 'time'

% IDENTITY
TIME [- 8]

An alternative, Murdoch thought, could be found in continental Europe. She remembered back in 1945 a Brussels bookseller thrusting into her hands a book called **Being and Nothingness** by someone called Jean-Paul Sartre. She was thrilled by the book and briefly met the author soon after. 'His presence in the city was like that of a pop star', she said later.

Meeting Sartre

Jean-Paul Sartre (1905-80) was not a pop star (though he could, according to former lover Simone de Beauvoir, do a great 'Ol' Man River'), but the closest thing to it even in France, a country that reveres philosophy almost as much as cuisine. Famous for his activities in the Resistance during the war, he was, ever since, a constant presence in the bars of the Left Bank in Paris, where he'd talk philosophy to anyone who fancied a beer.

It was only a single meeting... but it had a great bearing on Murdoch's own thought. Reading Sartre's philosophy, called existentialism, made the inadequacies of British philosophy stand out even more. She described his work as an inspiration to those (like her) who felt 'they must, and *could*, make out of all that misery and chaos a better world... Existentialism was the new religion, the new salvation'.

Existentialism:
the new religion

SO WHAT IS EXISTENTIALISM... AND WHY WAS IT SO POPULAR?

'People found in Sartre the clear and inspiring explanation of the world that philosophers are supposed to provide. The fundamental and attractive idea was freedom' (Murdoch). If we thought we'd had it bad after the war, this was nothing compared to the French. Imprisoned in their own country by the Nazis, with all the guilt and anger this unleashed, eternally fed up with the oppressive bourgeois systems of power... a philosophy that empha-sized *freedom* was bound to catch the French imagination. The result was that philosophy hit the streets like never before.

Existentialism is a philosophy about... well, existence. Starting from cer-tain facts about how we do live, it goes on to suggest how we ought to live.

...KEEPS ON ROLLIN'... ALONG! THANK YOU! NEXT WEEK: HEIDEGGER'S 'BEING & TIME'.

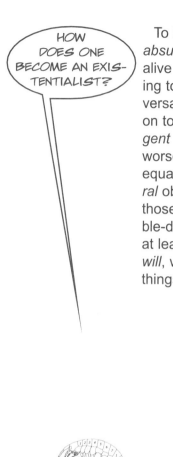

HOW DOES ONE BECOME AN EXISTENTIALIST?

To begin with, we must recognize that life is *absurd*, that is, entirely meaningless. We are alive for no reason, there is no purpose or meaning to our lives, we just *are*. Nor is there any universal framework of values that we can fall back on to give meaning to our lives. We are *contingent* (that is, unnecessary). To make matters worse we are surrounded by objects that are equally contingent (and here Sartre means *natural* objects, like trees or pebbles, which, unlike those we make ourselves—like paper, or a pebble-dashed wall—have no function.) While we are at least blessed with a *consciousness* and a *will*, we have to live in a world full of things that mostly have neither.

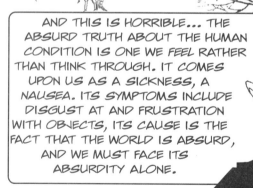

AND THIS IS HORRIBLE... THE ABSURD TRUTH ABOUT THE HUMAN CONDITION IS ONE WE *FEEL* RATHER THAN THINK THROUGH. IT COMES UPON US AS A SICKNESS, A NAUSEA. ITS SYMPTOMS INCLUDE DISGUST AT AND FRUSTRATION WITH OBJECTS, ITS CAUSE IS THE FACT THAT THE WORLD IS ABSURD, AND WE MUST FACE ITS ABSURDITY ALONE.

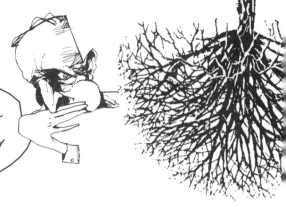

SO WHAT IS THE CURE FOR NAUSEA? HOW DO WE DEAL WITH IT? A COUPLE OF PARACETAMOL AND AN EARLY NIGHT? COMMIT SUICIDE? GET RELIGION?

No. We must understand its implications. We are free, nothing is holding us down. It is up to each one of us, in other words, to determine what we are and how we live. No other person, no pre-existing theory can help us.

MAN IS NOTHING BUT THAT WHICH HE MAKES OF HIMSELF. THAT IS THE FIRST PRINCIPLE OF EXISTENTIALISM.

WE ARE CONDEMNED TO BE FREE.

We may be 'thrown' into existence without any character or goals but this means it's up to us to create them. And we must do this by acts of 'pure decision'. To respond positively to our freedom—to live *authentically* as Sartre puts it—is to realise that life is a continual process of *making choices*. We must always be aware of the particular situation out of which choices arise, think through their consequences, before trying to make the right choice.

Of course, having to choose all the time might lead to a completely different kind of sickness... but once we accept the absurdity of the world, we cannot opt out: existentialism is a job for life. Freedom is not optional, it's a fact not a value. As Sartre said,..

29

Existentialism interested Iris Murdoch for several reasons:

• here was a philosophy much more ambitious that anything currently on offer anywhere else. It was *more* than a philosophy—it was 'a guide-book to living';

• its success had much to do with the artistic side of Sartre, the way he dramatizes his philosophy in novels and plays as well as essays;

• most of all, perhaps, she thought that much in Sartre's picture of the strange absurdity of the human condition was true. We are contingent. Life *is* absurd. There is no God...

In 1953 Iris Murdoch published the first book on Sartre in English, **Sartre: Romantic Rationalist**, (it is also her own first book). It was an immediate success. Soon the academic corridors of Britain were crowded with trendy bouffant-haired *philosophes* providing the answer to any philosophical question quicker than you can say 'hell is other people'. Murdoch's book on Sartre was one of the very early efforts to bring continental philosophy past the stuffy customs points of British thought.

Murdoch's book was a spirited introduction to existentialism. But it revealed there were also many things she *disliked* about Sartre. Her disagreements played as important a role as her enthusiasm in developing her own philosophy:

OKAY. I ACCEPT THAT WE ARE THROWN INTO AN ABSURD WORLD, FULL OF ALIEN OBJECTS AND OTHER PEOPLE THAT HAVE NOTHING TO DO WITH US.

BUT WHY SHOULD WE FIND THIS NAUSEATING? WHY NOT DELIGHT IN IT? ISN'T THERE SOMETHING EXCITING ABOUT OTHERNESS, ABOUT MYSTERY, ABOUT STRANGE OBJECTS? AFTER ALL, WRITERS HAVE BEEN DELIGHTING IN THIS FOR YEARS...

GLOBE TERESTRE

The strangeness of the everyday world we take for granted is something her own novels are especially clever at conveying. Some of her characters are startled, for example, by a sudden shrieking noise in their homes, only to realise it's the telephone.

31

Murdoch takes issue with other aspects of existentialism:

★ FIRST, ITS EMPHASIS ON THE SELF. 'HELL IS OTHER PEOPLE', SAYS SARTRE, BECAUSE OTHER PEOPLE, WITH THEIR OWN DESIRES AND OWN FREEDOM, COMPROMISE OUR OWN ATTEMPTS TO BE FREE. THIS VIEW IS SURELY UNHEALTHY—LIKE HIS IDEA OF NAUSEA, IT'S A THIN DISGUISE FOR SARTRE'S PERSONAL HANG-UPS;

★ SARTRE IS MORE INTERESTED IN IDEAS THAN PEOPLE. HIS WORK PLACES TOO MUCH EMPHASIS ON 'SYSTEM-BUILDING', TRYING TO GATHER EVERYTHING UP IN ONE THEORY;

HANG-UPS? MOI?

★ EXISTENTIALISM—LIKE ASPECTS OF LIBERAL HUMANISM, WHICH IT'S VERY UNLIKE IN OTHER WAYS—MAKES TOO MUCH OF HUMAN REASON AND THE WILL. IT IMPLIES THAT A PROBLEM CAN BE SOLVED SIMPLY BY THINKING, BEING DETERMINED TO SOLVE IT. IT FAILS, IN OTHER WORDS, TO TAKE ACCOUNT OF THE IRRATIONAL, MYSTE-RIOUS FORCES THAT MOTIVATE US.

While it offers something more than contemporary British philosophy, then, existentialism also shares its weaknesses. Liberal humanism, logical positivism, linguistic philosophy, and existentialism, the dominant post-war European philosophies, all present 'far too shallow and flimsy an idea of human personality'. They portray man as totally free, capable of self-knowl-edge, completely responsible for all his actions. In fact, when you come to think about it, Murdoch suggests, this is the main weakness of about 200 years of modern philosophy!

The contingent

Though existentialism had taken a wrong turn, at least it had started out on the right road... Its term **contingency** was one Murdoch adopted for her own use.

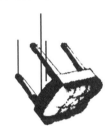

BUT FOR ME THE **CONTINGENT** ISN'T JUST WHAT IS 'NOT NECESSARY', IT'S ALSO WHAT'S 'UNPLANNED', OR ACCIDENTAL. FOR ALL HIS UNDERSTANDING OF HOW ABSURD EXISTENCE IS, THIS IS SOMETHING SARTRE DIDN'T TAKE ENOUGH ACCOUNT OF.

Life is governed by accident. We can't just plot our own course through life because we're not in control of everything. Chance events, and the desires of other people, may get in the way.

Yet we find this very difficult to accept. We want the world to make sense. What this means is that we want to be at the centre of our own world. So we have a strong desire to misread random accidental events as something significant. Or we try to *organize* chance events into a meaningful pattern. We want everything to make sense and for *us* to be meaningful too.

33

Murdoch insists that this desire is natural. Nor is it always a bad thing. (After all the instinct to shape things into a pattern produces some of our valuable social systems like politics and education, not to mention art.) Yet we have to be wary of it, because it can lead us to place too much importance on ourselves.

This desire to master the contingent is what Murdoch saw running right through existentialism. It's why Sartre chose to see contingency as something to provoke anxiety rather than wonder.

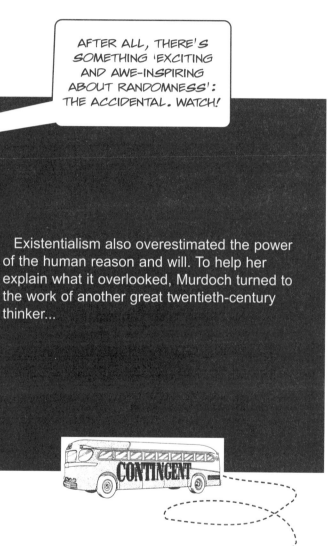

AFTER ALL, THERE'S SOMETHING 'EXCITING AND AWE-INSPIRING ABOUT RANDOMNESS': THE ACCIDENTAL. WATCH!

Existentialism also overestimated the power of the human reason and will. To help her explain what it overlooked, Murdoch turned to the work of another great twentieth-century thinker...

Freud

Sigmund Freud (1856-1939) was the inventor of *psychoanalysis*, the form of psychotherapy where talking about one's problems in the right way, and with the right kind of guidance from the analyst, promises to relieve them. He called it 'the talking cure'. According to Freud...

THE MIND IS SPLIT INTO TWO MAIN PARTS. THERE'S THE *EGO*, THE *CONSCIOUS* MIND WHERE WE THINK WE CONTROL OUR ACTIONS, AND EXERCISE REASON TO DO SO. THEN THERE'S THE *ID*, WHICH REPRESENTS THE *UNCONSCIOUS*.

The term 'id' is derived from the German for 'it', and it does suggest something monstrous. It's 'the dark, inaccessible part of our personality... a chaos, a cauldron full of seething excitations'—a mass of raw passions and desires. These exist in the unconscious mind, emerging only in a form acceptable to the ego and to the demands of the external world.

WHAT OUR CONSCIOUS MIND FINDS IMPOSSIBLE TO DEAL WITH—A TRAUMA, FOR EXAMPLE—GETS REPRESSED INTO THE UNCONSCIOUS, AND EMERGES IN ODD WAYS, MAINLY THROUGH DREAMS, SLIPS, AND JOKES. IT IS THE JOB OF PSYCHOANALYSIS TO DEAL WITH THIS REPRESSION THROUGH THE 'TALKING CURE'.

Murdoch disliked the therapeutic dimension of psychoanalysis. The danger is that the shrink has too much power, that he comes to function as a kind of megalomanic priest. Her novels often include just such a character. One, for example, Palmer Anderson in **A Severed Head**, justifies seducing a patient (strictly against psychoanalytic protocol, of course) by telling her:

But what Murdoch *likes* about Freudianism is its valid picture of the endless human capacity for *self-deception*. Though the Ego seems like the 'true' self, as it's the part that's involved in the real world, it's function is really to *disguise* what is going on in the seething cauldron deep within us all.

Psychoanalysis offered support for Murdoch's view that human beings *naturally* tend to be selfish. We love to create fantasies and fictions to console ourselves into thinking we're the centre of the world. We then become so convinced by our imaginings that we come to believe in them absolutely. We turn chance events into ominous signs. We fail, in other words, to acknowledge reality: 'Obsession shrinks reality to a single pattern'. This isn't quite as dramatic as it sounds. Murdoch simply means that...

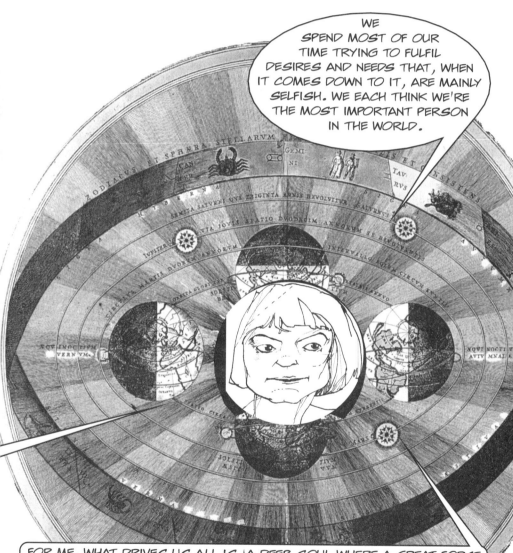

WE SPEND MOST OF OUR TIME TRYING TO FULFIL DESIRES AND NEEDS THAT, WHEN IT COMES DOWN TO IT, ARE MAINLY SELFISH. WE EACH THINK WE'RE THE MOST IMPORTANT PERSON IN THE WORLD.

FOR ME, WHAT DRIVES US ALL IS 'A DEEP SOUL WHERE A GREAT FORCE LIVES, AND THIS FORCE IS SEX AND LOVE AND ALL KINDS OF DESIRE—FOR POWER, KNOWLEDGE, GOD'. IT'S 'WHAT MAKES US GOOD OR BAD', IT'S WHERE ART AND SCIENCE SPRING FROM. IN SHORT, IT'S FAIRLY POWERFUL. I CALL THIS FORCE **EROS**—A NAME I TAKE FROM THE WORK OF MY FAVOURITE PHILOSOPHER, PLATO, WHO WE'LL MEET LATER.

Eros

Eros, Murdoch suggests, is best imagined as a kind of scale, moving from one extreme to another. At the bottom end of the scale are those base, animal desires that we experience most obviously as sexual arousal, and that prompt us to do many things, some touching, some ridiculous, some downright depraved.

DOWN AT THIS LEVEL IT'S ALL ABOUT DESIRE FOR OTHER PEOPLE, OR FOR ESSENTIALLY SELFISH AND POTENTIALLY DANGEROUS THINGS LIKE POWER AND POSSESSION.

AT THE TOP OF THE SCALE IS THE 'DIVINE EROS', WHERE THESE DESIRES ARE DIRECTED TOWARDS MORE NOBLE THINGS, THINGS OUTSIDE THE SELF, LIKE KNOWLEDGE, TRUTH, GOD, BEING GOOD.

Falling in love again (and again)

The characters in Murdoch's fiction are always acting in impulsive or bizarre ways because of erotic desire and what gets in the way of it. *A Severed Head*, for example, a novel much less like a horror movie than it sounds, is famous for the way its characters play a kind of 'musical chairs' with relationships:

Martin is married to Antonia but having an affair with Georgie. When he finds out that Antonia's been having an affair with Palmer, her psychoanalyst, his world is so shattered that he falls in love with Palmer's sister, the mysterious and demonic Honor Klein. On his way to tell her this, he is stopped in his tracks as he finds her in bed with... Palmer (her brother). During the course of the novel he finds out that his own brother Alexander has had an affair with Antonia and is having one with Georgie. He seems to achieve happiness at the end with Honor, while Georgie ends up with... Palmer.

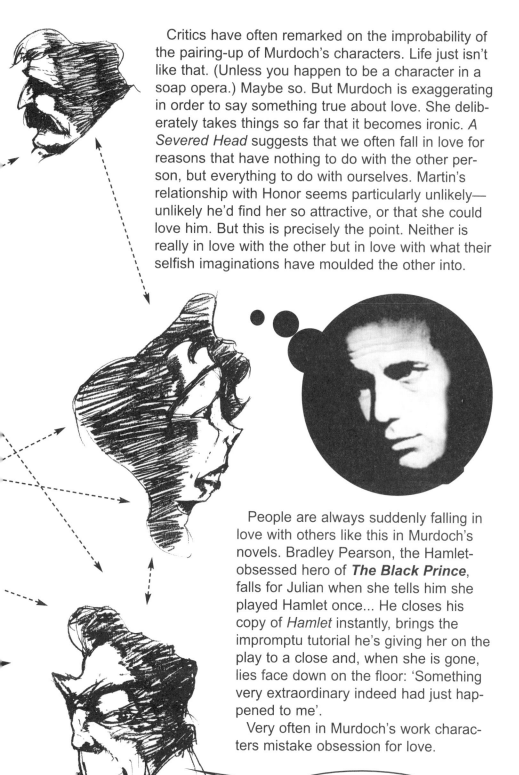

Critics have often remarked on the improbability of the pairing-up of Murdoch's characters. Life just isn't like that. (Unless you happen to be a character in a soap opera.) Maybe so. But Murdoch is exaggerating in order to say something true about love. She deliberately takes things so far that it becomes ironic. *A Severed Head* suggests that we often fall in love for reasons that have nothing to do with the other person, but everything to do with ourselves. Martin's relationship with Honor seems particularly unlikely—unlikely he'd find her so attractive, or that she could love him. But this is precisely the point. Neither is really in love with the other but in love with what their selfish imaginations have moulded the other into.

People are always suddenly falling in love with others like this in Murdoch's novels. Bradley Pearson, the Hamlet-obsessed hero of **The Black Prince**, falls for Julian when she tells him she played Hamlet once... He closes his copy of *Hamlet* instantly, brings the impromptu tutorial he's giving her on the play to a close and, when she is gone, lies face down on the floor: 'Something very extraordinary indeed had just happened to me'.

Very often in Murdoch's work characters mistake obsession for love.

I DID THAT ONCE. IT WAS FANTASTIC !

Summary

To summarize so far, then, Iris Murdoch is not a Christian, but the notion of Eros she derives from the dubious Freud and the divine Plato, gives her philosophy a kind of 'original sin':

- Human beings are contingent and our lives are determined by accident;

- We avoid recognizing this because of our natural selfishness and need for self-consolation.

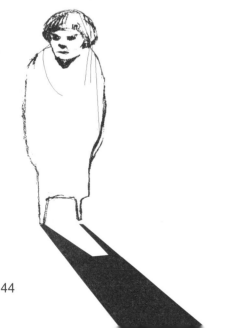

THIS IS THE FIRST STAGE IN MY ATTEMPT TO RE-THINK THE SHALLOW NOTION OF THE HUMAN PERSONALITY PROVIDED BY TWENTIETH-CENTURY PHILOSOPHY.

At the end of the 1950s, Iris Murdoch had become established as one of the most important figures in British culture. Her first two novels were quickly followed by **The Sandcastle** (1957), in which an affair between a schoolteacher and a young artist takes place against a background of dramatic events like cars falling in rivers and people falling off towers. Next came **The Bell** (1958), one of her most successful books. It expands on the themes central to her first two novels. It opens with an escape...

Dora Greenfield left her husband because she was afraid of him. She decided six months later to return to him for the same reason...

...and features an isolated religious retreat whose inhabitants are prevented from leaving by various kinds of 'enchantment'. It takes the moral questions (about guilt and betrayal, good and evil) that are subtly present in *Under the Net* and *The Flight from the Enchanter* and makes them more central: its plot revolves around a basically good man, a teacher, whose homosexual relationship with a basically self-centred and damaged man—who happens to be one of his pupils—later results in this man's suicide.

In a couple of very influential essays published at the end of the 1950s, '**The Sublime and the Beautiful Revisited**' and '**Against Dryness**', Murdoch compared the weaknesses of contemporary philosophy to the state of contemporary fiction. It was difficult to imagine any other literary critic even attempting to do the same, never mind being able to carry it off.

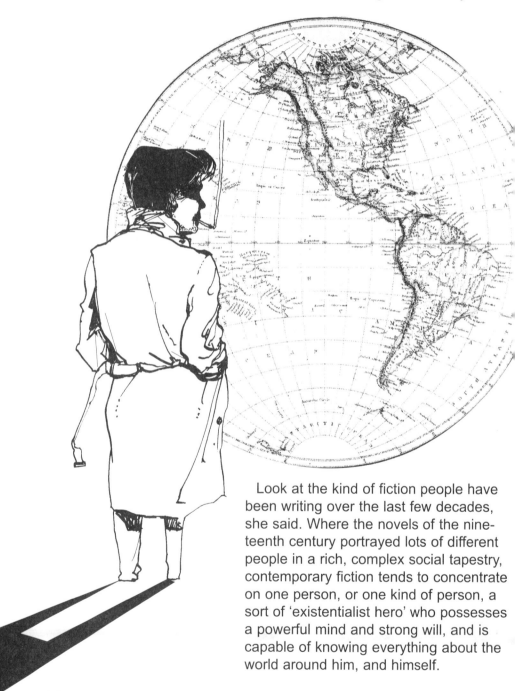

Look at the kind of fiction people have been writing over the last few decades, she said. Where the novels of the nine-teenth century portrayed lots of different people in a rich, complex social tapestry, contemporary fiction tends to concentrate on one person, or one kind of person, a sort of 'existentialist hero' who possesses a powerful mind and strong will, and is capable of knowing everything about the world around him, and himself.

WHAT IS MISSING FROM CONTEMPORARY FICTION AS A RESULT IS A PROPER SENSE OF REALISM. LIFE IS FULL OF THINGS THAT ARE MYSTERIOUS AND INEXPLICABLE—BUT THERE'S NO ROOM IN THE EXISTENTIALIST HERO'S WORLD FOR ANY OTHER POINTS OF VIEW, FOR ACCIDENT, FOR THE IRRATIONAL.

REALISM IS THE DOCTRINE THAT ART SHOULD AIM TO REPRESENT THE WORLD AND PEOPLE AS THEY REALLY ARE. AS SHAKESPEARE PUT IT, ART SHOULD 'HOLD A MIRROR UP TO NATURE'.

Realism in fiction is best seen in the great nineteenth-century 'classic' novels—even though they don't feature real people who actually existed, the characters are so accurately presented they, and the world that surrounds them, might just as well have been real.

What Murdoch especially liked about realism was that it enables the novelist to blend together the two aspects of fiction she thought were most crucial, **form** and **character**, in the most natural way—without one being more important than the other.

For Murdoch, form essentially means

1. **plot**: the way a story is organized and told;

2. **symbolism**: its deeper aspects, like images and repeated events, which come to stand for more than these things.

IN PARTICULAR I LOOKED TO THREE LITERARY 'GODS' (AS I LIKE TO CALL THEM) WHO COULD CREATE A RANGE OF VASTLY DIFFERENT CHARACTERS WHO BECOME ALMOST INSTANTLY 'REAL' TO US OFTEN IN JUST A FEW LINES OF PROSE, NO MATTER THEIR GENDER, SOCIAL STATUS OR AGE, WHILE ALSO IMPOSING A FORM ON THEIR WORKS THAT DID NOT REDUCE THESE CHARACTERS SIMPLY TO IDEAS DRESSED UP AS PEOPLE:

• the great English poet, playwright and Elizabethan man of mystery **William Shakespeare** (1564-1616);

• **Count Lev Nikolaievich Tolstoy** (1828-1910), a.k.a. Leo Tolstoy, probably the best nineteenth-century Russian writer;

• **Henry James** (1843-1916), an American writer who settled in Europe and shared many of Murdoch's moral concerns.

The Bell represented Murdoch's first proper effort to try to update the realist techniques of these authors into something suitable for the post-war times in which she lived. With its detailed realistic world full of different people, and its powerful symbolic undercurrent (the bell of the title is not just a bell, of course, it's a symbol) it's governed by what was to become Murdoch's *ultimate aim* as a novelist:

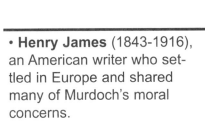

I WANT TO COMBINE MAGICAL PATTERN AND REAL PEOPLE THE WAY THE WRITERS I MOST ADMIRE DO.

The 1960s consolidated Murdoch's position high up in the literary intelligentsia, despite her preference for staying out of the limelight. She never did much of the journalism offered to important writers, and was rather uncomfortable appearing on television.

There was no let up in her extraordinary productivity as she threw herself into the task of developing her own form of realism. From 1961 to1971 Murdoch wrote an astonishing ten novels—almost one novel a year: *A Severed Head* (1961); *An Unofficial Rose* (1962); *The Unicorn* (1963); *The Italian Girl* (1964); *The Red and the Green* (1965); *The Time of the Angels* (1966); *The Nice and the Good* (1968); *Bruno's Dream* (1969); *A Fairly Honourable Defeat* (1970); *The Accidental Man* (1971).

Some writers spend years between novels. Iris Murdoch started planning her next novel as soon as she had delivered the previous manuscript to her publisher (usually in an old plastic shopping bag).

She was once asked...

...she replied.

The quality of her '60s books, it must be said, isn't always up to standard, though they're still wonderfully readable and deep, and some stand alongside her best work. In the 1960s what were to become familiar (and unfair) criticisms about Murdoch's work began to surface.

SHE WRITES TOO MUCH TOO QUICKLY, AND THE QUALITY IS SUFFERING.

WHY WON'T SHE ALLOW SOMEONE TO EDIT HER BOOKS?

It's true that she always refused to allow publishers to edit her books—one tried but was politely but firmly asked to put everything back the way it was.

HER NOVELS ARE TOO INTELLECTUAL.

SHE PRODUCES NOTHING MORE THAN POPULAR ROMANCES.

When asked, on the appearance of each new Murdoch novel, whether it was worth reading, **Ivy Compton-Burnett** (another novelist) used to reply:

DON'T BOTHER!

Philip Larkin (the shy jazz-loving misanthrope Murdoch remembered from Oxford) called each new novel...

THE SHITE FROM THE ENCHANTER.

BLAH BLA BLAH BL BLA BLAH BL E BL

But Murdoch was never one to bother much about critics. More important to her was the development of her writing—and also of her philosophy. While producing the great stream of '60s novels, Murdoch had continued to teach philosophy, moving in 1963 from her Oxford job to one at the Royal College of Art in London. Still occupying her mind was the need to devise a valid alternative to British liberal humanism and Sartrean existentialism.

ROYAL COLLEGE OF ART, PLEASE

It emerged most clearly in three long essays she published from 1964 to 1969 and which were collected in **The Sovereignty of Good**, published in 1970, a concise, elegantly-written statement of her philosophical position. This might be seen as the second stage of her re-thinking of contemporary philosophy.

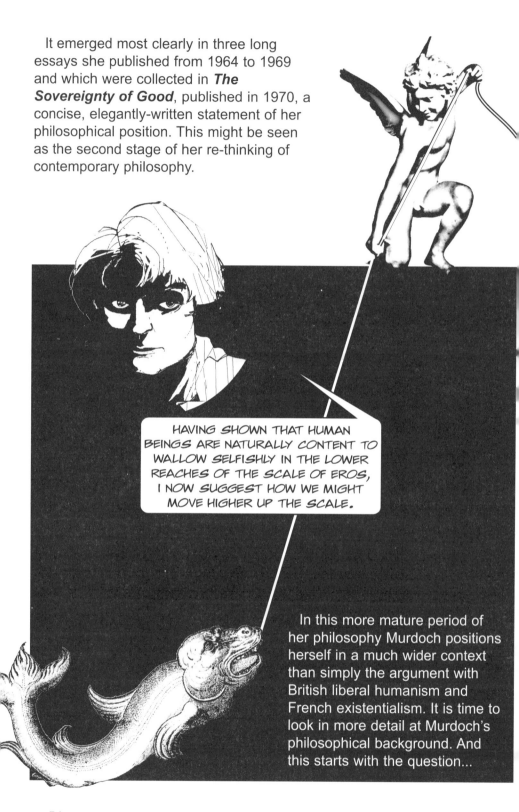

HAVING SHOWN THAT HUMAN BEINGS ARE NATURALLY CONTENT TO WALLOW SELFISHLY IN THE LOWER REACHES OF THE SCALE OF EROS, I NOW SUGGEST HOW WE MIGHT MOVE HIGHER UP THE SCALE.

In this more mature period of her philosophy Murdoch positions herself in a much wider context than simply the argument with British liberal humanism and French existentialism. It is time to look in more detail at Murdoch's philosophical background. And this starts with the question...

What kind of philosopher was Iris Murdoch?

Asking this question of a philosopher is a bit like asking someone to define in a sentence what the meaning of life is. Murdoch tended to answer it with tongue firmly in cheek:

> WHAT KIND OF PHILOSOPHER AM I? THAT'S SIMPLE. I'M A WITTGENSTEINIAN NEO-PLATONIST!

Philosophy is a vast subject, with a history almost as long as history itself, and is divided into many different areas. Murdoch's novels are full of philosophers who find doing philosophy very *difficult* (they often urge disciples not to get caught up in it). When she herself was asked where she would advise a newcomer to philosophy to begin, she answered that it wasn't necessary to begin it at all.

> PHILOSOPHY IS EXTREMELY OBSCURE AND BAFFLING. BUT THERE ARE SUCH WONDERFUL THINGS WRITTEN BY PHILOSOPHERS...

But Murdoch's thinking does fall into two main philosophical 'schools', **moral philosophy** and **metaphysics**.

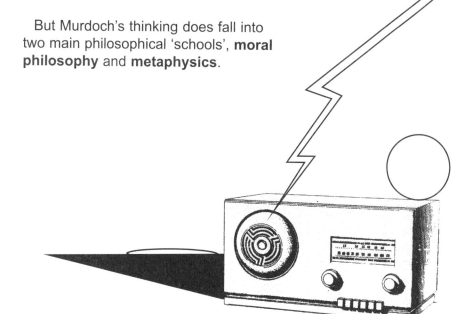

Moral philosophy

Moral philosophy concentrates on *ethical* questions:

- ○ **how do we act and how ought we to act?**

- ○ **what do moral words (like justice) mean?**

- ○ **how do we define key moral concepts (good, evil, right, wrong, etc.)?**

- ○ **where does moral behaviour come from—the reason or the emotions?**

- ○ **is morality a social or an individual thing?**

Moral philosophy has a long and distinguished history, and most of the most important philosophers there have ever been have made contributions to the debate.

Ancient Greece, the beginning of modern philosophy...
Aristotle (384-322BC), intellectual demi-god, argues...

> MORALITY IS ALL ABOUT 'EDUCATING' OUR EMOTIONS SO THAT WE CAN ACT APPROPRIATELY IN A GIVEN SITUATION (THE WAY A 'VIRTUOUS MAN' WOULD)...

The Enlightenment, early eighteenth century...
David Hume (1711-1776), said to be a 'virtuous man' (even though he entered politics), is convinced that

> MORAL BEHAVIOUR SPRINGS FROM TWO KINDS OF PASSION: SELF-INTEREST AND SYMPATHY FOR OTHERS.

Immanuel Kant (1724-1804), perhaps the most important Enlightenment philosopher (if not the most boring to read) disagrees:

> MORALITY IS NOT ABOUT FEELINGS BUT REASON. IT'S A MATTER OF DUTY—ONE ACTS FOR DUTY AND DUTY ALONE.

G. W. F. Hegel (1770-1831) adds his Kronigsworth: Kant's abstract view of duty ignores social interaction, the influence of other people.

MORALITY COMES FROM VALUES, CUSTOMS, FEELINGS WE ALL INSTINCTIVELY SHARE.

The next great phase of Enlightenment moral philosophy...

The **utilitarians**—(mainly two eminent Victorians, **Jeremy Bentham** (1748-1832) and **John Stuart Mill** (1859-61)—think the debate should move beyond considering the origins of moral action and imagining abstract moral situations. Morality comes down to one question, they insist: 'What's the most important thing in the world?' (it's a good question).

...AND THE ANSWER, OF COURSE, IS HAPPINESS. COULDN'T YOU GUESS?

Jeremy Bentham (1748-1832)

John Stuart Mill (1859-61)

'The way to be sure if a moral act is desirable or not is to decide whether it is likely to ensure "the greatest happiness for the greater number" ' (Bentham).

The twentieth century...

Moral concerns are still important, but few philosophers directly attempt to take ethical debate further than the Enlightenment.

Instead, moral philosophy becomes an ingredient in some of the most important intellectual schools: e.g. *psychoanalysis*, *Marxism*, and *existentialism*.

At the time when Murdoch was teaching philosophy, British moral philosophy reflected the weaknesses of other post-war philosophy. By getting bogged down in questions about language...

HOW CAN YOU SAY YOU ARE RIGHT WHEN YOU DON'T KNOW WHAT 'RIGHT' IS?'

...moral philosophy had argued itself out of the aim it once saw as central (as in utilitarianism, for example, which Murdoch admired) of offering people a guide for living.

I WANTED TO RETURN THIS FUNCTION TO MORAL PHILOSOPHY, AS WELL AS RETURNING ETHICS TO A PLACE OF IMPORTANCE IN PHILOSOPHY AS A WHOLE. TO ACHIEVE THIS, I ATTEMPTED SOMETHING RADICAL TO TRY TO SPARK MORAL PHILOSOPHY INTO LIFE: I INJECTED IT WITH A HEAVY DOSE OF METAPHYSICS.

METAPHYSICS

MORAL PHILOSOPHY

Metaphysics

'Metaphysical' literally means *beyond* or *after* the physical. It first got this name... well, the book that came after Aristotle's book on physics needed a name, but, more significantly, because metaphysics deals with the world beyond the physical world of experience.

Metaphysics deals with reality, but in a different way from the kind of philosophy that analyses the real, tangible things we can see, use or touch (e.g. linguistic philosophy, political philosophy, analytical philosophy, etc.). Metaphysics is the kind that asks any question of reality that cannot be answered via empirical (whatever we know, we know because of our senses) or scientific method.

It concentrates on things we experience, but which are more abstract, like time and space, substance, free will. The metaphysician is more likely to ask 'what is identity?' than 'what is the identity *of this particular thing*'. He or she investigates the world by a process of rational *conceptual* argument—or mystical intuition—rather than direct engagement with the material world.

Another key concern of metaphysics is the framework of concepts built up (either consciously or implicitly) by a particular philosophical approach. It analyses how philosophers think—metaphysics, in a way, is philosophy about philosophy.

Because of its concern with abstract or 'idealistic' questions metaphysics has long been a controversial area of philosophy. David Hume once said (not very virtuously) that any book of metaphysics should be 'committed to the flames' because it was nothing but...

SOPHISTRY AND ILLUSION.

It has received a particularly bad press in the twentieth century. Contemporary philosophy more or less accepts—following Nietzsche— that...

WE NO LONGER BELIEVE IN THE GREAT METAPHYSICAL SYSTEMS BY WHICH SOCIETY PREVIOUSLY FUNCTIONED.

In contemporary philosophy, as Murdoch says, 'God, Reason, Society, Improvement and the Soul are being quietly wheeled off'.

After the war, for everyone—logical positivists, linguistic philosophers, even existentialists—metaphysics is Philosophical Enemy Number One. But to Murdoch it's clear that the metaphysical is precisely what moral philosophy needs to get it back on track.

METAPHYSICS, IS INEXTRICABLY LINKED WITH MORAL PHILOSOPHY FROM THE VERY START. WHAT ARE CONCEPTS LIKE GOOD AND EVIL, FREEDOM, HAPPINESS, ETC. IF THEY'RE NOT METAPHYSICAL?

THAT'S FIGHTING TALK!

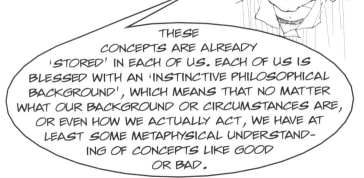

THESE CONCEPTS ARE ALREADY 'STORED' IN EACH OF US. EACH OF US IS BLESSED WITH AN 'INSTINCTIVE PHILOSOPHICAL BACKGROUND', WHICH MEANS THAT NO MATTER WHAT OUR BACKGROUND OR CIRCUMSTANCES ARE, OR EVEN HOW WE ACTUALLY ACT, WE HAVE AT LEAST SOME METAPHYSICAL UNDERSTANDING OF CONCEPTS LIKE GOOD OR BAD.

To support her argument, she turned to her philosophical hero, **Plato**.

The divine Plato

We know very little about Plato's life. We know he was born in 429 BC and died in 347 BC. We know that he was born in Athens, was of aristocratic origin, and was the star pupil of another great Ancient Greek philosopher Socrates. We know from his work that he wasn't too fond of artists (we'll see why soon) and that he thought philosophers, not politicians, should rule the ideal civilisation. Well he would say that, wouldn't he?

Of all the ancient Greeks, Plato has perhaps the best claim to be seen as the Father of Modern Philosophy. It was famously said that the entire body of Western Philosophy is nothing more than footnotes to Plato. All of the major issues debated by philosophers since, in other words, simply build on dilemmas clearly set out in Plato's work. He is certainly the first *metaphysician* of note.

IN FACT, FOR ME, PLATO IS METAPHYSICS AND METAPHYSICS IS PLATO, AND THAT'S ALL THERE IS TO IT.

OH... COME ON MARTIN, STOP IT PLEASE.

Martin Heidegger
German philosopher

Plato believed that there were two worlds

THE WORLD OF APPEARANCE;
THE WORLD OF REALITY.

But in a dazzling move, he *reversed* the way this might normally seem to us. The world of appearance is what we know as the 'real world', the one in which we drive home from work, grab a beer, and collapse in front of the TV. The world of reality, on the other hand, was somewhere else, somewhere beyond the physical, material realm of existence. This is the world that is *really* real for Plato—even though it's a purely intellectual world, quite distinct from the physical world.

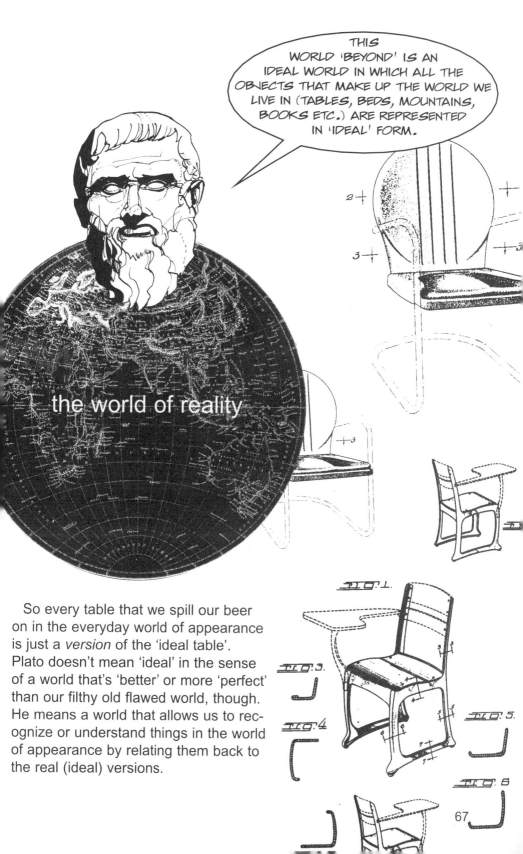

the world of reality

So every table that we spill our beer on in the everyday world of appearance is just a *version* of the 'ideal table'. Plato doesn't mean 'ideal' in the sense of a world that's 'better' or more 'perfect' than our filthy old flawed world, though. He means a world that allows us to recognize or understand things in the world of appearance by relating them back to the real (ideal) versions.

67

This is what's known as Plato's **theory of forms**. Whereas some philosophers see ideas as *concepts*, Plato sees them as *forms*, which have a distinct kind of representation—i.e. their own shape. It's the world of the forms that allows meaning to occur because the forms provide a kind of device by which we can measure our efforts to say or do things in the everyday world.

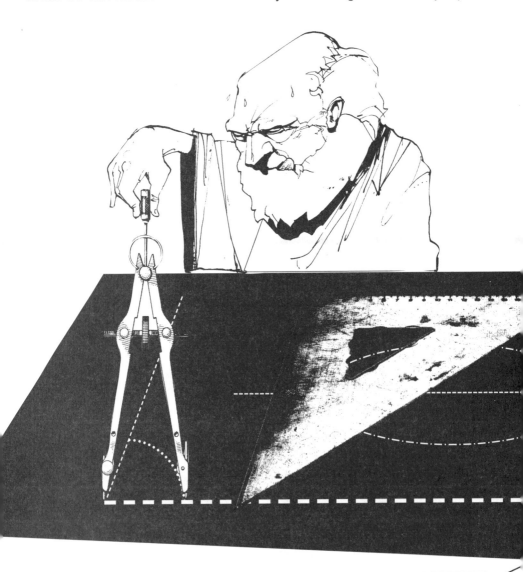

DRAWING A LINE WITH A PENCIL AIMS TO PRODUCE A STRAIGHT LINE, BUT OF COURSE IT CAN NEVER BE PERFECTLY STRAIGHT. IT DOES, HOWEVER, EVOKE AND IS CAUSED BY THE ESSENTIAL IDEAL OF 'STRAIGHTNESS'. WE KNOW WHAT IT'S SUPPOSED TO BE. AND SO WHEN SOMEONE FAILS TO DRAW A STRAIGHT LINE, WE AT LEAST KNOW WHAT THEY WERE TRYING TO DO—IT'S THE FORM THAT MAKES THE ACT INTELLIGIBLE.

This is straightforward enough for tables and pencils. But what about more complex things, like *concepts*? Actually, the same principle holds true. In fact, the capacity of the forms to enable meaning is perhaps most relevant when it comes to abstract metaphysical ideas. Instead of comparing a line someone has drawn with the ideal form of a straight line...

This is Plato's metaphysics. And what excited Murdoch about it was that it could be used to create a kind of 'metaphysics as a guide to morals' (as the title of her last and most ambitious work of philosophy put it) urgently required by the godless twentieth century.

'Metaphysics as a guide to morals' or: a theology without God

Many of Murdoch's characters experience extreme guilt.

Edward Baltram in **The Good Apprentice** (1985), for example, feels that his life is destroyed after he gives his friend Mark LSD as a joke. Mark thinks he can fly, jumps out of the window, and dies. Edward is treated mercifully by the courts, but his punishment is worse: he receives continual hate-mail from Mark's mother reminding him of his guilt.

GRADUALLY, THOUGH, AS TIME PASSES, I AM READY TO REPENT. I AM READY TO BECOME AN APPRENTICE LEARNING HOW TO BE GOOD. BUT THE PROBLEM IS: I DON'T BELIEVE IN GOD. I DON'T EVEN BELIEVE IN MORALITY.

The problem of morality in a world without God is one that Murdoch's 'metaphysics as a guide to morals' is designed to confront. It argues that we can preserve the invaluable metaphysical concepts in religion—good, selflessness, forgiveness, etc.—while getting rid of the more dubious parts of religion.

IN PARTICULAR, I SEE NO DISADVANTAGE IN DITCHING THE IDEA OF A PERSONIFIED FATHER-FIGURE CALLED GOD.

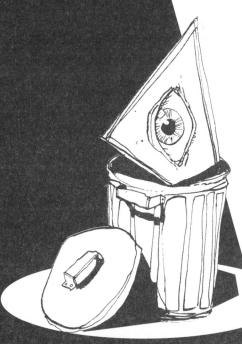

Murdoch liked the idea of a kind of 'metaphysical utilitarianism', something 'less optimistic and more desperate' than the philosophy of Bentham and Mill. Setting out the basic requirements for human beings, the original utilitarians obviously meant essentials like food and shelter. But why couldn't that be extended to metaphysical things like 'freedom, democracy, truth and love'?

This is one of the things Murdoch liked about Sartre. Though on the surface he's one of the most anti-metaphysical philosophers of all, Murdoch points out that he relies upon one metaphysical picture throughout his work: *freedom*. In a way, Sartre's philosophy itself offers a kind of 'metaphysics as a guide to morals'. It paints a vivid picture of our contingent position in an absurd world, and suggests how an adherence to an *idea* (freedom) could help us deal with this.

In the same way that Sartre uses freedom, Murdoch talks about Good. This is her neo-Platonic alternative to religion: God is replaced as the focal point by Good.

Saying we can have a religion without God is controversial, of course. It also seems to make no sense—like saying we can have a meal without food.

YET A RELIGION DOESN'T HAVE TO HAVE A GOD. ONE OF THE RELIGIONS I ADMIRED MOST WAS BUDDHISM, AN ATHEIST RELIGION.

The pilgrimage from appearance to reality

In 1977 Murdoch wrote more directly than she'd ever done about her interest in Plato. The result is one of her best books of philosophy, beautifully presented and passionately argued: **The Fire and the Sun**.

The title comes from Plato's famous story about the cave. This story is at the heart of Murdoch's philosophy, and often referred to in her fiction.

LET'S HEAR THE STORY.

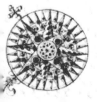

Then, later, they manage to escape into the outside world, which they see in the natural light of the sun. Eventually—and this is the last stage on their journey—they find themselves able to look at the sun itself.

The story of the cave is about a 'pilgrimage from appearance to reality'. It illustrates the need to move from what Plato called *eikasia* (the state of delusion) to the state of enlightenment.

In Plato's theory of forms, *the good* is in fact the most important form of all. It's present in the world, yet—being a metaphysical concept—not in the way that trees are present in the world. It is exhibited in actions and, more rarely perhaps, people. In the allegory of the cave the sun represents the form of goodness. To undertake a moral pilgrimage towards goodness is to renounce the confined world of images and emerge from the cave and see that the world is illuminated by the light of the good. Recognizing real goodness is not easy, however, but something we have to *learn* to do. As Murdoch says...

IT'S DIFFICULT TO LOOK AT THE SUN.

THE JOURNEY FROM APPEARANCE TO REALITY IS WHAT I THINK PLATO'S WHOLE PHILOSOPHY IS ALL ABOUT, NOT TO MENTION EVERY GOOD PLAY AND NOVEL. BUT IT ALSO APPLIES TO MY OWN PHILOSOPHY AND FICTION. MY WORK CONSTANTLY STRESSES THE IMPORTANCE OF MOVING FROM A CONDITION OF SELF-CENTRED IGNORANCE TO ONE OF ALTRUISTIC ENLIGHTENMENT, WHERE THE EXISTENCE OF OTHERS IS PROPERLY RECOGNISED.

Murdoch's fiction depicts the pilgrimage from appearance to reality—usually the failure of this pilgrimage—in endlessly imaginative ways. Most often it does so by depicting the struggle between the *artist* and the *saint*. If there's one theme that can be seen as central in every one of Murdoch's novels this is it.

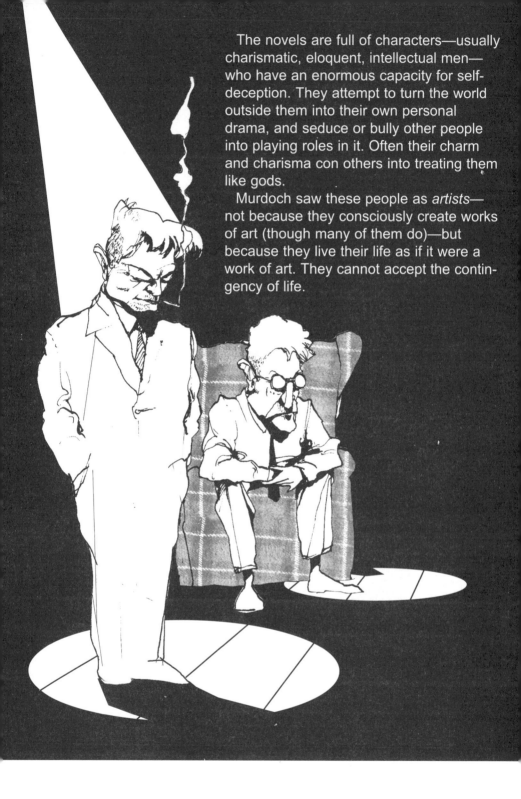

The novels are full of characters—usually charismatic, eloquent, intellectual men—who have an enormous capacity for self-deception. They attempt to turn the world outside them into their own personal drama, and seduce or bully other people into playing roles in it. Often their charm and charisma con others into treating them like gods.

Murdoch saw these people as *artists*—not because they consciously create works of art (though many of them do)—but because they live their life as if it were a work of art. They cannot accept the contingency of life.

Julius King, in *A Fairly Honourable Defeat* (1970), is one example of an artist. He's a version of Murdoch's enchanter figure, who acts as a kind of mad stage manager in everyone else's life. He sets out—for no apparent reason, other than to satisfy his own need to manipulate others—to destroy the marriage of Rupert and Hilda, and succeeds ruthlessly. The break-up leads to Rupert's death.

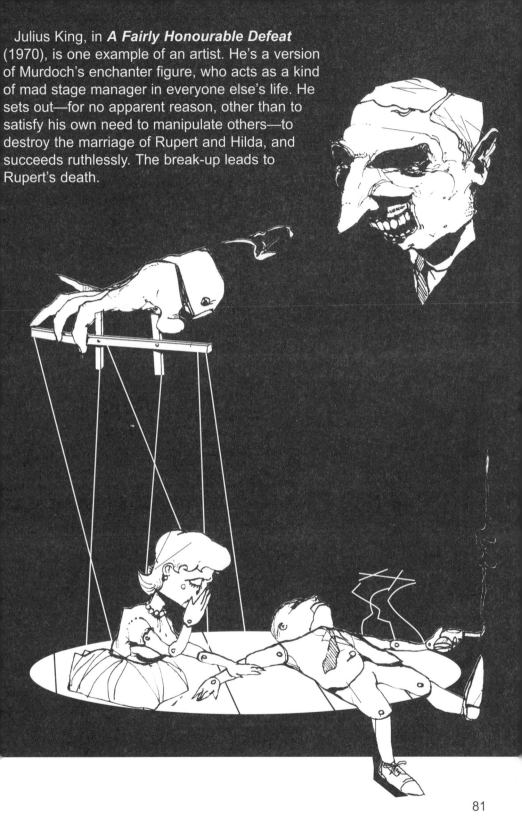

Julius is opposed by a completely different kind of character, Tallis Browne. Tallis is chaotically untidy where Julius is scrupulously clean, reflecting his ability to live with contingency. He is only too aware of the dangers of artistically arranging his life. Though his marriage has also failed, he tries throughout to respect other people and to be good.

Tallis Browne represents the *saints* in Murdoch's work. It has to be said, though, that they don't look much like saints. They're usually very ordinary, sometimes shabby people, leading very mundane lives. But this is Murdoch's point. It's more attractive to try to dramatize one's life than to try to be good.

The devil always gets the best tunes. This also results in a particular dilemma for a novelist, as Murdoch recognises. Julius King, one of her most interesting characters, asks:

WHAT NOVELIST EVER SUCCEEDED IN MAKING A *GOOD* MAN INTERESTING?

Tallis courageously tries to stand up to Julius, but he's no match, and Julius wins. But his defeat is a 'fairly honourable' one.

The opposition of artist and saint reflects how closely Murdoch's fiction and philosophy are intertwined, without either being subservient to the other. It subtly reminds us of what her philosophy makes more explicit, that we must avoid giving in to the temptation to become artists.

But this doesn't mean that we should try to become saints. Murdoch knew how unlikely this was—as she was often mistaken for one.

I INSISTED ON ANSWERING THE HUNDREDS OF LETTERS I GOT EACH WEEK PERSONALLY AND BY HAND. MOST OF THE MONEY I MADE FROM THE HUGE SALES OF MY NOVELS I GAVE AWAY, SOMETIMES HANDING LARGE ROYALTY CHEQUES STRAIGHT TO CHARITIES.

Trying too hard to be a saint could also defeat the purpose. Stuart Cuno in **The Good Apprentice** gets on everyone's nerves sitting around all day just contemplating goodness. Instead we should embrace the otherness of the world—its randomness and mystery—without trying to relate it to ourselves.

The Seventies

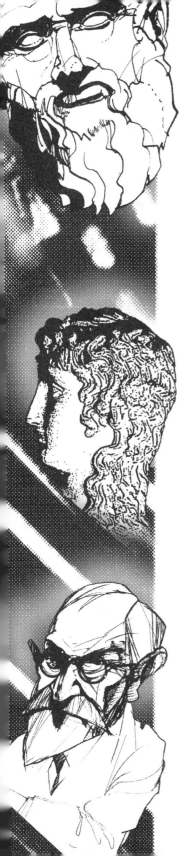

Published in 1970, **A Fairly Honourable Defeat**, begins the decade when Murdoch, after a period of hits and misses, fulfils her early potential as a writer. Like its successor, **An Accidental Man**, it has an assurance in dealing with large casts and deep subject matter that her previous novels were unable to sustain to quite the same degree. These two books are followed by a succession of her best novels: **The Black Prince** (1973), which many readers and critics acclaim as her most brilliant; **The Sacred and the Profane Love Machine** (1974), which wins the prestigious Whitbread Prize for Fiction; **A Word Child** (1975), and **Henry and Cato** (1976), published in the same year Murdoch is awarded a CBE (Commander of the Order of the British Empire) medal. Her last novel of the Seventies caps her 'great decade' by moving her fame to a new level. In 1978 **The Sea, the Sea** wins the most important British fiction prize of them all, The Booker Prize. The Booker is often a source of controversy, but it always results in massively increased sales and readership for the winning author, and increased critical respect.

Murdoch's 1970s novels explore the complex nature of Eros. *The Black Prince* and *The Sea, the Sea* are moving and comic studies of obsessive love, while *Henry and Cato* features a doubtful priest contemplating the love of God. Eros explains the curious title *The Sacred and the Profane Love Machine*. 'Sacred' refers to Plato's 'divine' Eros, 'profane' to the more base 'Freudian' version. Both kinds of energy are expended in equal measure throughout the book.

The 1970s novels are also preoccupied with the role of contingency and accident in human life. The hero (though he's not very heroic) of *An Accidental Man*, Austin Gibson Grey, finds his life changed when he accidentally kills a little girl while driving his car drunk. Hilary Burde in **A Word Child** causes the death of his lover by becoming so angry driving on the motorway that he speeds over the central reservation.

Both novels are subtle Murdochian cautionary tales...

Hilary's response to Anne's death is to immediately cut short a glittering career as an academic and do a mundane office job instead. He shapes his life into a rigid pattern, always doing the same thing at the same time on the same day. He passes his evenings on the Circle Line on the London Underground going round and round, stopping nowhere.

What he thinks he's doing is punishing himself, and protecting against accident intervening in his life again and causing more pain. He feels that the crash was the result of 'the gods' persecuting him for previous sins. What he's *actually* doing, however, is weaving around the contingent events of his past one of the those self-centred fictions Murdoch warns about. He tries to make a tragic random occurrence seem part of a grand design. Hilary's aim to punish himself by giving up a rewarding future is just another form of self-gratification.

Being good (for nothing): mysticism

Murdoch once said that ' "All is vanity" is the beginning and the end of ethics. The only genuine way to be good is to be good "for nothing" '. In the 1950s she first came across the work of one of the most remarkable women of our time, **Simone Weil**, a French thinker. Though, like Murdoch, she drew on existentialism and Plato, Weil's work was difficult to fit into the various schools of philosophy. This is because she wasn't really a philosopher. She was a *mystic*. And a mystic, though it sounds more like an astronomer or a fortune-teller, is simply, Murdoch said, 'a good person whose knowledge of the divine and practice of the selfless life has transcended the level of idols and images'.

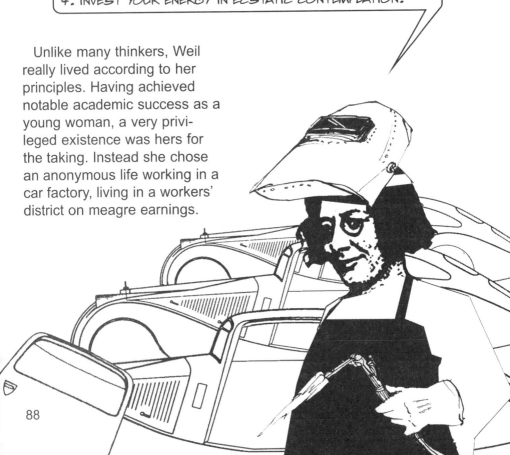

HOW TO RENOUNCE EVERYTHING AND BECOME A MYSTIC?
1. KILL THE SELF;
2. DECREATE NOT RECREATE;
3. RENOUNCE BOTH THE PAST AND THE FUTURE, FOR BOTH INVOLVE AN ATTACHMENT TO AN IMAGINARY SELF;
4. INVEST YOUR ENERGY IN ECSTATIC CONTEMPLATION.

Unlike many thinkers, Weil really lived according to her principles. Having achieved notable academic success as a young woman, a very privileged existence was hers for the taking. Instead she chose an anonymous life working in a car factory, living in a workers' district on meagre earnings.

Then, like many of the more politically motivated intellectuals of the time (such as George Orwell), she went to help the left-wing cause in the Spanish Civil War (though she was no more affiliated to a political party than she was to a particular philosophical 'school'). She never used her weapons and concentrated on 'animating' those she worked alongside.

Eventually, forced to live in London during the Nazi occupation of France, she starved herself to death in sympathy with the plight of her fellow Jews back home.

Ascesis

Weil's life and work embodied a key concept for Murdoch—what the ancient Greeks called *ascesis*, a form of rigorous self-discipline and abstinence from self-gratifying pursuits. As well as mysticism, the ascetic temperament is particularly associated with *religion*. It's fundamental in Buddhism, but also features in Christianity, which urges us to renounce or at least temper the pleasures of the flesh.

HEY, BABY! WHAT YOU GOT UNDER THAT CASSOCK?

NOTHING BUT PURE MORAL FIBRE, LOVE.

ONE FOR THE ROAD, BISHOP?

ONLY IF IT'S THE ROAD TO SPIRITUAL ENLIGHTENMENT.

Murdoch didn't think we should starve ourselves to death like Simone Weil, though, or give up material comforts and live in a cave like a hermit. She valued educating ourselves to focus our energies on the needs or desires of other people. This will lead, she suggests, to an unexpected bonus, whereby we actually find our own self greatly nourished as a result.

THE BEST WAY TO HELP YOUR-SELF IS TO HELP SOMEONE ELSE.

Unselfing is a central concern of her novels, where it features in two main ways. One is where characters like Tallis Browne or Stuart Cuno try to contemplate goodness. The other is much more dramatic: where a character is taught an ascetic lesson by some kind of mythical fate.

One of Murdoch's favourite Greek myths, which she often used in her novels, relates to the ideal of ascesis: the story of **Apollo** and **Marsyas**.

Apollo is the god of art and the muses. He is the one to whom all aspiring and even accomplished artists should look for guidance.

Marsyas is a mortal, the inventor of a beautiful double-flute.

He challenges Apollo to make music on his lyre as enchanting as his flute.

Apollo accepts on one condition: whoever wins can inflict any punishment on the loser.

(And when a god makes a proviso like that, you know you're in trouble.)

The first duel is a draw. For the next, Apollo challenges Marsyas to play his flute upside down.

Marsyas is declared the loser.

As a punishment Marsyas is tied to a pine tree and flayed alive by Apollo—the skin is literally peeled off.

93

As a result of his excessive pride, Marsyas is *unselfed* in a horribly literal way. Murdoch retells this story in her own way in *The Black Prince*, where Bradley Pearson, one of her most self-obsessive—but strangely endearing—heroes, is punished for treating other people simply as objects in his world when he's framed for a grisly murder. He is thrown in prison—symbolically 'skinned', punished for being too wrapped up in himself.

Attention

Mystics like Simone Weil seek to achieve congress with the *divine*.

> THIS MIGHT SOUND LIKE A LOT OF FUN BUT IT'S ABOUT THE ARDUOUS PROCESS OF FINDING A PATH TO ENLIGHTENMENT THAT HAS NOTHING TO DO WITH REASON.

Mystics seek a kind of knowledge that isn't about facts and ideas. The key is to make ourselves no longer ourselves by paying attention to things *outside* ourselves. This is done through **ecstatic contemplation**.

> ECSTASY LITERALLY MEANS 'STANDING OUTSIDE YOURSELF'.

Murdoch insisted that the verb 'to see' always has a moral connotation. It is very important to look *fairly* at the world around us, at the people around us, and the particular situation we find ourselves in.

WE MUST REALISE WHY WE BEHAVE AS WE DO IN A PARTICULAR SITUATION. WE MUST REGISTER HOW OUR ACTIONS MIGHT AFFECT OTHER PEOPLE INVOLVED.

This is precisely what many of Murdoch's characters *don't* do. In **Under the Net** Jake Donahue is too wrapped up in himself to make sense of what's right in front of his eyes. He's convinced that Anna loves him and Sadie loves his friend Hugo, when it's obviously the other way round. Murdoch gently teaches her hero a lesson by making him eventually realise this.

A term Murdoch admired in Simone Weil's work is '*attention*'. Attention is a bit like religious worship. When we pray we direct our attention to some entity whose existence can help us. In Christianity this entity is God. Murdoch describes God as...

> A SINGLE PERFECT TRANSCENDENT NON-REPRESENTABLE AND NECESSARILY REAL OBJECT OF ATTENTION.

> WHAT?

> IT'S ANOTHER WAY OF SAYING THAT HE EXISTS EVEN THOUGH HE CANNOT BE SEEN. GOD IS PRESENT EVEN THOUGH HE IS ABSENT.

For religious people God can be 'seen' in the work of good people, in the existence of beautiful things, in the workings of nature.

One of Murdoch's favourite passages in the Bible was: 'Whatsoever things are true, whatsoever things are honest, whatsoever things are just, whatsoever things are pure, whatsoever things are lovely, whatsoever things of good report... think on these things.'

GOODNESS

INSTEAD OF GOD, I PREFER US TO DIRECT OUR ATTENTION TOWARDS SOMETHING ELSE THAT EXISTS IN THE WORLD WITHOUT BEING DIRECTLY VISIBLE, SOME OTHER METAPHYSICAL FORCE THAT IS PRESENT YET ABSENT: *GOODNESS*.

But this is not as simple as it might sound. It requires dedication—merely looking at a few things now and then in a meditative manner won't relieve us of our problems. In *The Good Apprentice* Stuart, the irritating man who is trying to be good, advises the intolerably guilty Edward to...

LOOK AT THIS AZALEA PLANT TO RELIEVE THE BURDEN OR YOUR PAINED SELF

Edward replies:

OH GO AWAY, GO TO HELL, AND TAKE THE BLOODY PLANT WITH YOU OR I'LL TRAMPLE ON IT.

Nevertheless attention is crucial in the pilgrimage from appearance to reality.

Closely related is another important Murdochian term—though this one doesn't belong to any particular philosopher...

Love!

Murdoch said that 'falling in love is a violent process that is for many people the most extraordinary and most revealing experience of their lives. The centre of significance is suddenly ripped out of the self, and the dreamy ego is shocked into awareness of an entirely separate reality'.

Love was something she knew about. At Oxford in the early 1950s, recovering after the tragic loss of two lovers, Murdoch met **John Bayley**. He has said that from the moment he first saw her cycling past his window, he knew they would be married.

As the book Bayley published in 1998, *Iris: A Memoir*, shows (though not deliberately), his marriage to Iris Murdoch is a great love story. But it's great in precisely the way that it differs from the tempestuous romances of couples like Elizabeth Taylor and Richard Burton. (Great lovers don't normally buy their clothes from charity shops or languish in a famously squalid kitchen.)

THROUGHOUT OUR MARRIED LIFE WE WERE ALMOST INSEPARABLE—GOING ON ENDLESS LECTURE TOURS TOGETHER, VISITING FRIENDS ABROAD, SWIMMING IN WHATEVER KINDS OF WATER WE COULD FIND—AND ALWAYS CHILDISHLY HAPPY TOGETHER.

But before this all becomes too sentimental, we should remind ourselves that Murdoch knew all about the destructive power of love. Our self-centred tendencies often find their most extreme outlet in love.

Yet love also represents the ideal of *attention*. When we love someone—that is, when we *really* love someone (rather than just lusting after them or seeing them as someone who can improve our self-image)—we are really *seeing* them.

When we gaze lovingly at our partner, when we really consider what they've just said, when we reflect that their reaction to a particular situation is *just them* somehow, what happens?

WE BECOME SO IMMERSED IN THEM THAT WE ACTUALLY FORGET OURSELVES FOR A MOMENT. WE OBLITERATE OUR SELF BY ATTEMPTING TO EMPATHIZE WITH ANOTHER BEING.

THAT'S THE IDEAL, ANYWAY. TO APPLY THIS PRINCIPLE TO OTHER SITUATIONS IN LIFE DOESN'T MEAN WE HAVE TO LOOK AT EVERYONE WE MEET IN DEWY-EYED RAPTURE BUT SIMPLY THAT WE MUST STRIVE TO CONSIDER HOW OTHER PEOPLE ARE EXPERIENCING THINGS. WE REALLY HAVE TO IMAGINE WHAT IT'S LIKE TO BE THAT PERSON.

We can now look at one of the most distinctive aspects Murdoch's philosophy: the importance it attaches to *art*.

Plato was notoriously suspicious of art.

I KNOW THIS IS PARADOXICAL, BECAUSE MY OWN WRITING—IN WHICH I MASTER A DRAMATIC FORM, THE DIALOGUE—USES ARTISTIC DEVICES TO HELP ME PUT FORWARD MY VIEWS. BUT I OBJECTED ON MORAL GROUNDS:

•ART ENCOURAGES US TO EXPRESS OUR LOWEST AND MOST ANIMAL EMOTIONS, THE LOWER PART OF EROS IN OTHER WORDS.

IF PLATO WERE ALIVE TODAY HE WOULD CERTAINLY AGREE THAT WATCHING VIDEO NASTIES IS HARMFUL.

• BECAUSE ITS DUTY IS TO REPRESENT THINGS, ART IS ALWAYS DEALING WITH APPEARANCES NOT REALITY—AND REMEMBER WHAT I THINK OF APPEARANCES: EVEN IF WHAT IT REPRESENTS IS ESSENTIALLY GOOD, IT'S STILL PORTRAYED VIA THE LIGHT OF THE FIRE IN THE CAVE, NOT THE SUN OUTSIDE.

• WHAT'S MORE, THE CHARAC-TERS IN LITERATURE, DRAMA, AND OTHER FORMS OF ART ARE MORE LIKELY TO BE BAD PEOPLE BECAUSE THEY ARE MORE ENTERTAINING AND UNPRE-DICTABLE, WHEREAS GOOD PEOPLE ARE QUIET AND NEVER CHANGE.

• ART—EVEN GREAT ART—TENDS NOT TO BE CLEAR ENOUGH ABOUT ITS MORAL POSITION. IT'S MORE CONCERNED WITH SHOWING US THINGS AND LETTING US MAKE UP OUR OWN MINDS RATHER THAN TELLING US WHAT TO THINK, AND THIS IS RISKY.

107

For these reasons, Plato regarded artists as a bunch of sleazy liars, and chose to banish them from his ideal state.

Murdoch agrees with Plato's insights on art, but only up to a certain point. Art can seduce us into swallowing a consoling myth—one that actually tells a lie about the world.

Many artists use art as a kind of 'protective symbolism' that simply reflects back to them their own fantasies.

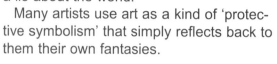

I AGREE THAT, BECAUSE IT OPERATES THROUGH EROS, ART IS CONCERNED WITH THE SENSES, IT MAKES US FEEL. BECAUSE IT AFFECTS US AT A DEEP LEVEL IT CAN LEAD US ONTO EXALTED PLANES...

...OR DISTURB US.

109

What's more, precisely because it shows rather than tells, art teaches in a different and more valuable way to other disciplines. After reading a great novel we may feel we can't say what it *means* but are equally convinced that we have benefitted somehow from reading it. Art can teach us a special kind of truth. 'Art can explain without revealing.'

THE EXPERIENCE OF ART IS ALWAYS A MORAL ONE.

ART IS ALL THE SAME QUALITY.

BUT SOME ART IS BETTER THAN OTHERS. AND JUST AS BAD ART CAN HAVE A NEGATIVE EFFECT ON US, GOOD ART CAN BE POSITIVE: IT IS GOOD FOR US WHEN IT IS GOOD AND BAD FOR US WHEN IT IS BAD.

111

GOOD ART TEACHES US HOW TO ATTEND TO THINGS PROPERLY. IT TEACHES US HOW REAL THINGS CAN BE LOOKED AT AND LOVED WITHOUT BEING TAKEN INTO THE GREEDY ORGANISM OF THE SELF.

Looking at a great painting is very similar to the experience of really looking at a person we love. We forget ourselves and for a moment 'become' the person in the painting, or come to experience the situation absolutely. It's close to a religious experience—we almost come to worship what we come into contact with.

HERE'S HOW TO USE MY PHILOSOPHY AS A GUIDEBOOK TO LIVING!

• Life is a journey from appearance to reality.

• 'Low Eros' is where we start from.

• Goodness is where we want to get to.

• Stripping away the self (ascesis) through ecstatic contemplation (the 'loving look' of attention)—is how we get there.

• Metaphysics is how we make sense of our journey.

The ascetic and the aesthetic

Murdoch brought art into her philosophy and her philosophy deeply influenced the way she created art.

She believed that there are two kinds of author. There are those who put themselves into their work to such an extent that the work is nothing but their personal fantasy or philosophy dressed up as art. These authors, to use a phrase in *The Black Prince*, 'empty themselves all over their world like scented bathwater'.

Often the kind of novel produced by these authors can be brilliant, enjoyable to read, sometimes even a masterpiece.

BUT IT'S NOT HOW ART SHOULD BE. I PREFER THE OTHER KIND OF AUTHOR, ONE WHO REVEALS VERY LITTLE OF HER PERSONALITY IN HER WORK AND MANAGES TO IDENTIFY WITH LOTS OF DIFFERENT KINDS OF PEOPLE, MANY OF WHOM ARE UNLIKE HER AND BELIEVE IN COMPLETELY DIFFERENT THINGS.

In short, this second kind of author is one who embodies Murdoch's philosophical ideal of ecstatic contemplation. This author attends properly to the world outside her, and 'loves' her characters selflessly. Murdoch's 'literary gods'—Shakespeare, Tolstoy and James—were all this kind of author.

And this is the kind of author Murdoch strove to be in her work. Her reluctance for details of her own life and character to be made public wasn't just to do with shyness, but with her convictions about writing.

I DON'T MIND HAVING A PERSONAL STYLE, BUT I DON'T WANT TO BE PRESENT PERSONALLY IN MY WORK. I WANT TO LET MY WORK SPEAK FOR ME.

   And this, more and more, is what she was content to do for the last two decades of her life. After the excitement of winning the Booker had died down, Murdoch gave fewer interviews and concentrated on producing a series of rich, absorbing novels. They appeared a bit less frequently than before—perhaps because they were becoming longer and longer. *The Sea, the Sea* was followed by seven further novels: **Nuns and Soldiers** (1980), **The Philosopher's Pupil** (1983), **The Good Apprentice** (1985), **The Book and the Brotherhood** (1987), **The Message to the Planet** (1989), **The Green Knight** (1993) and *Jackson's Dilemma* (1995).

These novels are twentieth-century equivalents of the great Victorian classics—teeming with characters all wrapped up in compelling plots. During this time she continued to be honoured by universities and societies around the world. *The Book and the Brotherhood* was also shortlisted for the Booker Prize. The greatest public recognition of all came when she was made a Dame of the British Empire in 1987—perhaps the highest public honour a British woman can receive. She accepted the award wearing plimsolls (to relieve her arthritis). The achievement was commemorated by the Phillips portrait.

In the painting Murdoch appears against a mythological, classical back-drop, which reflects the strange other-worldly quality of her fiction. There is something in her last novels of Shakespeare's last great plays, romances like *The Tempest* and *A Winter's Tale*, where an air of magic hangs over everything. Their world is very like the real world, but also a completely different place.

The four-year gap between *The Message to the Planet* and *The Green Knight*—longer than between any previous novels—was not the result of Murdoch's work rate or enthusiasm dimming, however. In 1992 she produced *Metaphysics as a Guide to Morals*, in which all her thinking about philosophy, the great philosophers, the role of art in our lives was rolled into one massive book, which took 10 years to write.

Though it's a bit of a chaotic jumble at times, it's a fitting crys-tallization of Murdoch's unique contribution to philosophy.

A quiet dark place

Sadly, there's another reason why the gaps between Murdoch's books began to grow in the 1990s.

In 1994, friends first began expressing concern about the author's health. She was rumoured to be going through a worrying writer's 'block'—most unusual for someone previously as prolific as Iris Murdoch. A couple of years later Murdoch's husband John Bayley informed the newspapers that she was suffering from Alzheimer's disease. She was unable to remember that she had written 26 novels and 5 books of philosophy, didn't know that she had been awarded the Booker Prize, or that she had been made a Dame of the British Empire, was unaware that she was regarded as one of the most important and original writers of the late twentieth century. She described her condition as being made to occupy 'a very quiet dark place'.

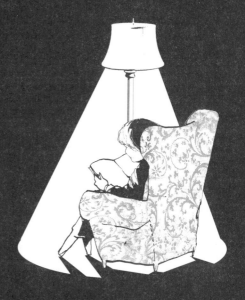

As her condition worsened she soon became quite unable to work. She died in Oxford on 8 February 1999.

It's not unusual for authors' deaths to spark off more interest in them than when they were alive. In the late 90s Murdoch once again became the subject of newspaper articles and academic 'reappraisals'. Yet her sudden decline into illness gave this interest a tragic slant: because she'd been forced to stop writing it was as if the obituaries were being written before she was dead. Her illness and death quickly made Murdoch famous in a different way—and in a wider cultural sphere than simply the literary and intellectual world where she had been best known throughout her life.

Part of this is to do with the horrible irony of her illness. It's almost impossible not to be struck by how terrible it is for such an obviously clever person, having devoted her life to knowledge and art, to end up unable to remember a single title of one of her books. Her story reminds us of one of the fundamental philosophical issues of all, one Murdoch herself spoke of in many different ways and on many different occasions:

NO MATTER WHAT WE SPEND OUR LIVES DOING, NO MATTER HOW FAMOUS WE BECOME, WE DO IT... FOR WHAT? THE GREAT NOTHINGNESS OF DEATH WILL ENVELOP US ALL.

Murdoch's growing status as a cultural icon was achieved, though, mainly by her husband John Bayley's very public attempts to deal with this issue. Just before she died he published a warm and moving tribute, *Iris: A Memoir* (called *Elegy for Iris* in the United States). Part biographical story, part sad account of a terrible decline into illness, the book was a huge success. It was a bestseller, serialized in the press, named by some critics as their 'Book of the Year'. One even called it 'the love story of our age'.

IRIS: A MEMOIR INCLUDES SOME FASCINATING BIOGRAPHICAL DETAILS ABOUT IRIS : HOW SHE AND I BECAME LOVERS WHEN SHE FELL DOWN THE STAIRS AT AN OXFORD DANCE AFTER TRIPPING ON HER SKIRT; HER STRANGE RELATIONSHIP WITH THE NOBEL PRIZE-WINNING AUSTRIAN WRITER ELIAS CANETTI, WHOM I CONFESS TO JEAL-OUSLY CALLING THE 'GOD-MONSTER OF HAMPSTEAD'; THE SURPRISING FACT THAT, ALTHOUGH SHE USUALLY NEVER SHOWED ANYONE HER WORK UNTIL IT WAS FIN-ISHED, IT WAS I WHO WROTE THE FAMOUS OPENING LINE OF THE BELL.

123

But Bayley's honesty also ensures his book reveals many painful, uncomfortable details about his wife's decline—not just her childlike mental state, but also her regressive physical condition. This made Bayley the object of much criticism from reviewers, which intensified as he published a follow-up, *Iris and the Friends*. Though none questioned his honourable motives for writing the books, his love for his wife, or the beautiful simplicity of his style, many found they were being told things they just didn't want to know about a great author, which seemed to diminish her literary importance by dwelling on her physical frailty.

This seems a little harsh, as there's much more to the books than this. The 'friends' of the second book, for example, are the precious memories, which turn out to be all he and Murdoch had at the end of their life together—perhaps all anybody has.

Yet what is indisputable is the fact that Murdoch is becoming known more and more for other things than her work. And this is ironic, for she was always very reluctant for her past and her character to become public property. She made sure that the events in her work couldn't simply be compared to events in her life. All this would be fascinating in the case of any writer. But it's particularly ironic when it comes to *this* one. Iris Murdoch was always suspicious of generalisations, but it's not too risky to say that her fiction, her philosophy, and even her life were all dominated by the idea of unselfing. How ironic, then, that her self should now be of so much interest.

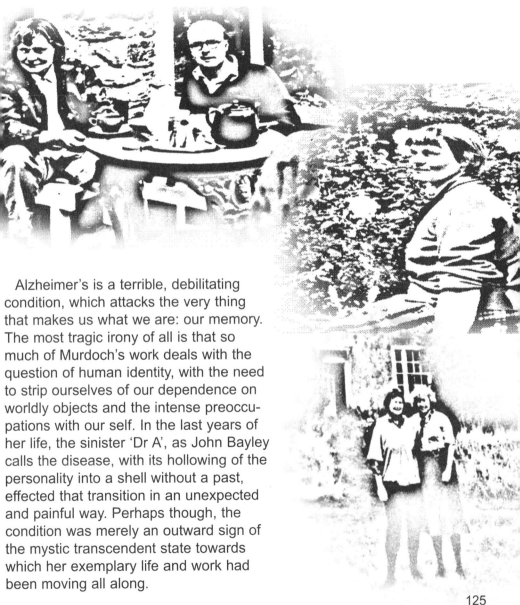

Alzheimer's is a terrible, debilitating condition, which attacks the very thing that makes us what we are: our memory. The most tragic irony of all is that so much of Murdoch's work deals with the question of human identity, with the need to strip ourselves of our dependence on worldly objects and the intense preoccupations with our self. In the last years of her life, the sinister 'Dr A', as John Bayley calls the disease, with its hollowing of the personality into a shell without a past, effected that transition in an unexpected and painful way. Perhaps though, the condition was merely an outward sign of the mystic transcendent state towards which her exemplary life and work had been moving all along.

'Perhaps the best that can be said, and that is indeed a great deal, is that the writer can and will in the end resemble the Buddhist master who said that when he was young he thought that mountains were mountains and rivers were rivers, then after many years of study and devotion he decided that mountains were not mountains and rivers were not rivers, and then at last when he was very old and wise he came to understand that mountains are mountains and rivers are rivers.' ('Existentialists and Mystics')

Further reading

Murdoch's fiction

Murdoch wrote 26 novels. Each one is an exciting and absorbing piece of entertainment, each intriguingly explores some of the issues set out in this book, any of them would be a good place to start reading Murdoch. But, for what it's worth, here's what I consider the very best of Murdoch's fiction:

Under the Net, London: Penguin, 1954
The Bell, London: Penguin, 1958
A Severed Head, London: Penguin, 1961
A Fairly Honourable Defeat, London: Penguin, 1970
The Black Prince, London: Penguin, 1973
The Sacred and Profane Love Machine, London: Penguin, 1974
A Word Child, London: Penguin, 1975
The Sea, the Sea, London: Penguin, 1978
The Philosopher's Pupil, London: Penguin, 1983
The Good Apprentice, London: Penguin, 1985
The Book and the Brotherhood, London: Penguin 1987
The Green Knight, London: Penguin, 1993
Jackson's Dilemma, London: Penguin, 1995

All are still in print; all are available in paperback.

Murdoch's philosophy

Sartre: Romantic Rationalist (reissued: London: Penguin, 1987). Though first published in 1953, this is still one of the best discussions of existentialism. It contains a more subtle exposition of Murdoch's developing philosophy.

The Fire and the Sun: Why Plato Banished the Artists (Oxford: Oxford University Press, 1977). Beautifully written and elegantly argued, this is one of the best introductions to Plato, and also Murdoch's quarrel with and extension of Platonism.

The Sovereignty of Good (reissued: London: Routledge, 1985). A concise, clear and thought-provoking statement of Murdoch's philosophical position.

Acastos (London: Penguin, 1987) is philosophy of a different kind: two Platonic dialogues first performed on stage in 1980, giving a dramatic and entertaining introduction to her neo-Platonist views on art and religion.

A more challenging—but at times very rewarding—read is Murdoch's major statement of her philosophical position, *Metaphysics as a Guide to Morals* (London: Chatto and Windus, 1992).

Murdoch's numerous articles and essays on philosophy stretching over some 40 years have recently been collected together in *Existentialists and Mystics: Writings on Philosophy and Literature*, edited by Peter Conradi, and published by Chatto and Windus, 1997.

Books about Iris Murdoch

There is very little in the way of biographical material on Iris Murdoch, though this has recently begun to change, sadly as a result of her illness and death. John Bayley's *Iris: A Memoir* (London: Duckworth, 1998) is a moving tribute to the author and a painful account of her illness, but also contains some funny and fascinating insights into her life. A. N. Wilson and Peter Conradi are currently writing the first full biographies of Murdoch.

Books about Murdoch's work are more common. The best introductory studies (apart from *Iris Murdoch For Beginners*, of course) are:

Peter Conradi, *Iris Murdoch: The Saint and the Artist* (2nd edition: London: Macmillan, 1989). A lucid and persuasive survey of almost the whole Murdoch canon.

Richard Todd, *Iris Murdoch* (London: Methuen, 1984). Short, readable general study.

Deborah Johnson, *Iris Murdoch* (Brighton: Harvester, 1987). Brings an unusual and welcome feminist slant to Murdoch criticism.

A.S. Byatt, *Degrees of Freedom* (reissued: London: Vintage, 1994). Includes Byatt's other writings on Murdoch.

Index

The authors

Bran Nicol—the unusualness of the first name and the apparently uncommon spelling of the surname (at least in England) mean that he has had numerous alternative names over the years, from the mundane to the bizarre—was brought up in Fife in Scotland. He currently teaches contemporary literature and theory at University College Chichester and his research is on neurosis and the contemporary novel—which he admits may be in some way autobiographical. He is the author of *Iris Murdoch: The Retrospective Fiction*. His favourite phrase is 'Caledonian antisyzygy'.

Piero is an accomplished illustator and graphic designer. He earned his degree at the Art University of La Plata, Buenos Aires and has had several published illustrations. His work has twice been included in the Royal College of Art's 'Best of British Illustration' (1998, 1999). He is currently studying animation at Westminster College in London.

**GARCÍA LORCA
FOR BEGINNERS®**
Luís Martînez Cuitiño
Illustrated by
Delia Cancela
ISBN 0-86316-290-8

US $11.95
UK £7.99

1998 marked the centenary of the birth of one of Spain's brightest stars in the fields of poetry and drama, Federico García Lorca. His poetry never goes out of print and his plays still have an impact on audiences throughout the world. Lorca or 'Federico', as he was known, was born in Granada in 1889 and was executed, without trial, at the age of thirty-eight by the Falange at the start of the Spanish Civil War.

Lorca was one of the most influential and talented members of the avant-garde movement of his generation. His chilling and com-pelling drama *Blood Wedding* established him as the dramatist who revived Spanish-speaking theatre.

Lorca appealed to all levels of Spanish society; he merged popular art forms such as gypsy songs and lyrics with classical poetry and music.

In **García Lorca for Beginners®**, Luis Martínez Cuitiño analyses Lorca's work within the context of his life—a life filled with passion and drama—while Delia Cancela's illustrations compliment the text by recreating the line and style of Federico's own drawings.

**RUDOLF STEINER
AND ANTHROPOSOPHY
FOR BEGINNERS®**
Lía Tummer
Illustrated by Lato
ISBN 0-86316-286-X

US $11.95
UK £7.99

At the dawn of the twentieth century Rudolf Steiner created Anthroposophy, the 'spiritual science' that opposes the blindly science-believing, materialistic ideology inherited from the previous century. In so doing, he introduced a truly humanistic concept. Based on a profound knowledge of the human being and his relationship with nature and the universe, Anthroposophy has not only been able to provide renewing impulses to the most diverse spheres of human activity, like medicine, education, agriculture, art, religion, etc., but is also capable of providing answers to the eternal questions posed by mankind, towards which the 'natural sciences' remain indifferent: what is life? where do we come from when we are born? where do we go when we die? what sense has pain and illness? why does some people's destiny seem unjust?

Rudolf Steiner and Anthroposophy for Beginners® describes this universal genius' solitary growth from a childhood in the untamed beauty of the Austrian Alps to the sublimities of human wisdom.

what's new?

**EASTERN PHILOSOPHY
FOR BEGINNERS®**
Jim Powell
Illustrated by Joe Lee
ISBN 0-86316-282-7

US $11.95
UK £7.99

Eastern philosophy is not only an intellectual pursuit, but one that involves one's entire being. Much of it is so deeply entwined with the non-intellectual art of meditation, that the two are impossible to separate.

In this accessible survey of the major philosophies of India, China, Tibet and Japan, Jim Powell draws upon his knowledge of Sanskrit and Chinese, as well as decades of meditation. Whether tackling Buddha, Confucius, Lao Tzu, Dogen, the Dali Lama or Patanjal—Powell's insights are deeply illuminating.

All the major philosophies of India, China, Tibet and Japan are explained and the spiritual rewards and intellectual challenges of Eastern philosophy are revealed in this visually stunning book.

This is an exceptionally beautiful **For Beginners®** book, with 19th-century engravings throughout.

Everyone—from beginner to expert—will find **Eastern Philosophy for Beginners®** a beautiful and insightful overview.

**PIAGET
FOR BEGINNERS®**
Adriana Serulnikov
Illustrated by
Rodrigo Suarez
ISBN 0-86316-288-6

US $11.95
UK £7.99

Jean Piaget's theory of intellectual development is a result of his life's work, spanning almost 80 years of study. His contribution to the field of child psychology is equal to that of Sigmund Freud's achievements in psychiatry. Piaget's aim was to find the answer to the epistemological question: how do you construct human knowledge? Or: how do you acquire precision and objectivity?

Through interviews and tests with children (including his own), Piaget and his colleagues studied the acquisition and development of knowledge in the course of childhood and adolescence, from which he developed his theory of genetic psychology. His work has inspired numerous studies in the fields of education and developmental psychology.

Piaget for Beginners® investigates the key moments of the scientist's life, which are also landmarks in his own personal and professional development.